REVISED EDITION

PLAYING the BASS GUITAR

A Beginner's Guide to the Electric Bass

by Verdine White and Louis Satterfield
with Karl Kaminski

AF009447

To access audio, visit:
www.halleonard.com/mylibrary

Enter Code
"3965-0131-5175-5388"

ISBN 978-1-60378-283-8

Copyright © 2012 Cherry Lane Music Company
International Copyright Secured   All Rights Reserved

No part of this publication may be reproduced in any form or by
any means without the prior written permission of the Publisher.

Visit Hal Leonard Online at **www.halleonard.com**

Explore the entire family of Hal Leonard products and resources

World headquarters, contact:
Hal Leonard
7777 West Bluemound Road
Milwaukee, WI 53213
Email: info@halleonard.com

In Europe, contact:
Hal Leonard Europe Limited
1 Red Place
London, W1K 6PL
Email: info@halleonardeurope.com

In Australia, contact:
Hal Leonard Australia Pty. Ltd.
4 Lentara Court
Cheltenham, Victoria, 3192 Australia
Email: info@halleonard.com.au

Contents

Foreword to the Revised Edition 3
Introduction 3
Dedication 3
History of the Bass Guitar 4
The Rudiments of Music 5
Introducing the Bass Guitar 10
Holding the Bass Guitar 13
Fingerboard Diagram 16
Playing the Open Strings 17
Notes on the First Three Frets 27
Slappin' Basics 35
Construction of Major Scales 40
Movin' On Up: Playing the 2nd, 3rd, and 4th Frets 48
Using Pentatonic Scales 58
Movin' On Up: Playing the 3rd, 4th, and 5th Frets 68
Thumpin' & Poppin' in Octaves 76
Movin' On Up: Playing the 4th, 5th, and 6th Frets 81
Movin' On Up: Playing the 5th, 6th, and 7th Frets 91
Movin' On Up: Playing the 6th, 7th, and 8th Frets 99
Syncopation 107
Movin' On Up: Playing the 7th, 8th, and 9th Frets 111
Additional Basic Slappin' Techniques 119
A Look at Minor Scales 122
Strengthening the Fingers 128
Verdine's Grooves 130

Foreword to the Revised Edition

Anyone familiar with Verdine White's bass playing will surely agree that he is a powerhouse of energy and freedom. As the bassist for Earth, Wind and Fire, he lays it down with the dexterity of an all-pro athlete!

With any endeavor, an organized approach is the key to success. In *Playing the Bass Guitar*, Verdine has laid out a systematic method to learning the basics of music theory and how it relates to your bass. By the end of the book, you'll not only understand and read music but you'll also gain the independence needed to move around your instrument with ease.

I hope you enjoy the book, and with the knowledge you gain, you'll come to know Verdine's freedom and spirit.

—Karl Kaminski

Introduction

Inspiration for writing *Playing the Bass Guitar* came from the great Louis Satterfield. At the time Louis and I released the first edition, there weren't many books on the market that primarily dealt with the bass guitar, music theory, and their relationship to pop music. Our main goal was—and is today—to show how wonderful the instrument is while demystifying the elements that not only relate to the bass, but to music in general. This book is a great way to learn the basics while allowing you to jump right in and start playing your music.

Learn the basics to build a foundation, and from there you can grow!

—Verdine White

Dedication

To all of the bass players all over the world and to Louis Satterfield, who taught me everything I know on the bass guitar!

Photo by Bruce W. Talamon

Louis Satterfield (1937–2004)

History of the Bass Guitar

The first known ancestor of the bass guitar was an early African rhythm instrument known as the *earth drum*. This simple instrument, made by staking an animal skin over a hole in the ground, displayed all the rhythmic and melodic principles of today's bass guitar. A string, tied from the center of the skin, was attached to a stick on the side of the hole and plucked with one finger. To change the pitch of the deep bass tones, the stick was moved back-and-forth to increase or decrease the tension.

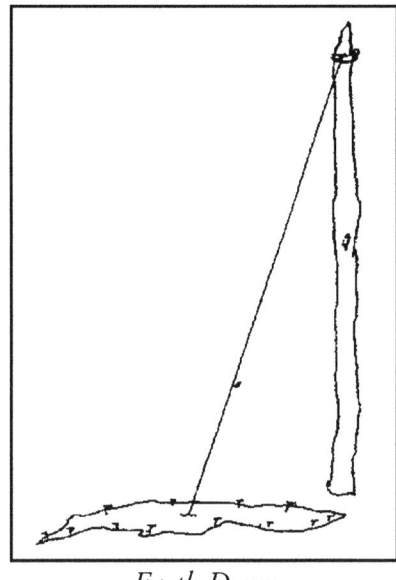
Earth Drum

The *washtub bass*, once common to Appalachian music, is also considered a forerunner of the modern bass. It was made from common household items: an inverted washtub, a pole, and a wire that connected the two. The washtub bass created a drum-like rhythmic feel while maintaining a basic bass line similar to today's electric bass.

The bass tuba and string bass provided the deep melodic rhythms for concert orchestras, as well as Dixieland, jazz, and marching bands. Both instruments were steps along the way to the modern bass guitar.

The invention of the electric guitar pickup and amplifier brought the bass guitar into prominence. Although the double bass and the bass guitar may differ in sound, their functions are essentially the same: to maintain a foundation in the string section of an orchestra or rhythm section of a band.

Leo Fender and Fred Tovares developed the first electric basses in the late 1940s. The Fender *Telecaster* and *Precision Bass* were on the market by the early 1950s and initially used by country artists Bob Willis and Charlie Ray (while Ray was playing with John Daum). Lionel Hampton and Monk Montgomery are credited with introducing the electric bass to the jazz world. The most notable debut of electric bass in a pop song was on Les Paul and Mary Ford's famous recording "How High the Moon."

To get a real "feel" for the bass, one should listen to a variety of bassists from different eras. Starting in the 1940s, you'll find the early jazz string bassists such as Slam Stuart, Wilbur Ware, Oscar Pettiford, and Ray Brown. From there, you'll find the more contemporary upright players like Charles Mingus, Ron Carter, Richard Davis, and Scott LaFaro.

In the 1950s, Monk Montgomery was one of the first upright bassists to pick up the electric bass—certainly, he was the first to use it in the jazz idiom. Some jazz bassists who deserve your listening attention include Stanley Clarke, Jaco Pastorius, and Alphonso Johnson—all inventive electric bassists. Other legendary electric players to be aware of are James Jamerson, Louis Johnson, Larry Graham, and Bootsy Collins. The evolution of the bass steadily continues with Marcus Miller, Victor Wooten, Flea, and Esperanza Spalding.

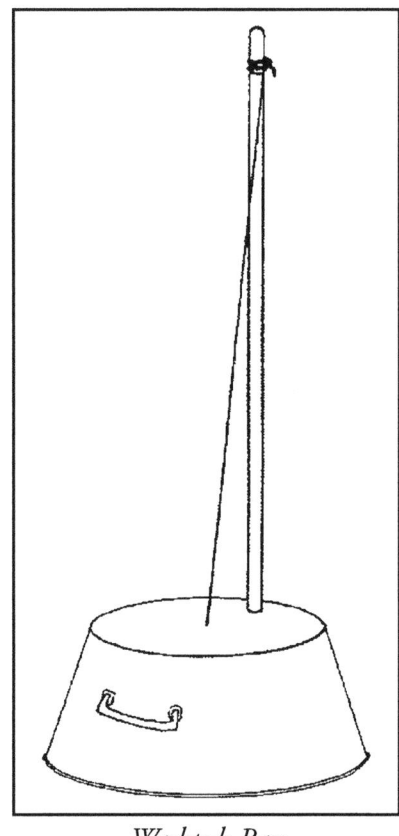
Washtub Bass

To achieve a good understanding of the vast variety of musical styles out there—past, present, and keeping an eye out for the future—listen to examples from the full musical spectrum. This should include symphonic works, music from India, gospel, jazz, music of the West Indies, and the funkiest of funk music. Listen carefully and sing what you hear and see. This approach will not only help your ear, but also your technical development, as you will be in immediate touch with the music. Remember: all musical instruments are nothing more than extensions of the human voice. You should be able to create and play what you are hearing and feeling by using your ears, voice, bass guitar, or any musical instrument. Then, the next step—developing your own personal style—becomes that much simpler.

The Rudiments of Music

Music is the art of combining sound in a manner agreeable to your ear. It can be divided into three main elements: melody, harmony, and rhythm. The first two elements deal with the *pitches*, or notes, that you hear.

A *melody* is a combination of notes that forms a tune. The notes can vary in pitch, duration, and succession to create horizontal movement in the music.

The second element, *harmony*, is the combination of notes vertically. When several melodies are simultaneously stacked on top of one another, their *intervals*—the distances between notes—create harmony.

The third element of music is *rhythm*. Rhythm is the duration of the pitches and sounds you make; it's the beat and the heart and soul of any groove! As a bassist, this is the most important element to master. Without it, you're not playin' music—you're just playin' *notes*.

Learning to read music is really simple. The first step is to be able to understand the symbols. Written music can be broken down into two parts: pitch and rhythm. Again, the pitches are the highs and lows of the notes, and the rhythm is how frequently you play the notes and for how long you sustain them. Let's take a look at the pitches first.

The "Musical Alphabet"

Just like any language, music has an alphabet, which consists of letters: A–B–C–D–E–F–G. The notes will repeat forwards or backwards but *never change order*. If we move up through the pitches, we would have: A–B–C–D–E–F–G, A–B–C–D–E–F–G, etc. Going down in pitch is just the reverse.

The Staff

Music notation is written on a *staff*. The staff consists of five lines with four spaces. The staff is broken up into measures via a *bar line*. The end of a section is notated with a *double bar line*. The example below contains two measures.

The Clef

The beginning of the staff contains a *clef*. The clef indicates a reference pitch for the staff. The *bass clef* indicates that the 4th line is an F (notice that the dots mark the 4th line). The bass clef is used for low-pitched instruments, including cello, bass guitar, bassoon, trombone, bass violin, and tuba.

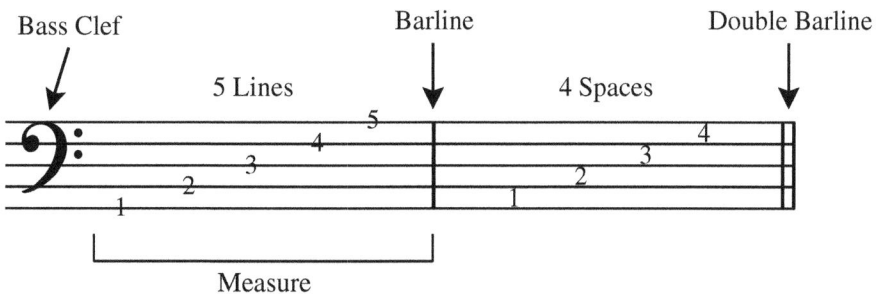

There are many ways to memorize the notes on the lines and spaces of the bass clef—you may remember some from elementary school. The easiest way to remember the order of notes is to construct a sentence with the pitches of the lines and another with the spaces. You can use the ones below or make up your own.

For the lines (G–B–D–F–A), you could use: **G**ood **B**assists **D**o **F**ine **A**lways.

For the spaces (A–C–E–G), you could use: **A**ll **C**ows **E**at **G**rass.

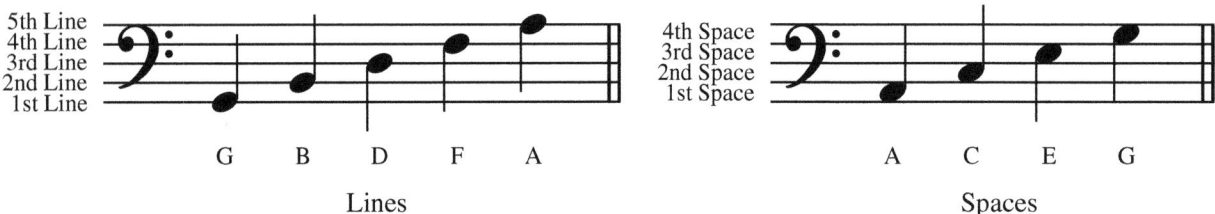

Notice that, if you start on the first space (A) and move up consecutively, line–space–line–space–line–space, it spells the alphabet (A–B–C–D–E–F–G), with the top line being A again.

Ledger Lines: Above and Beyond

Pitches can be written above or below the staff by means of short lines called *ledger lines.* The lowest note on your bass is an E. Notice that this note is found on the first ledger line below the staff.

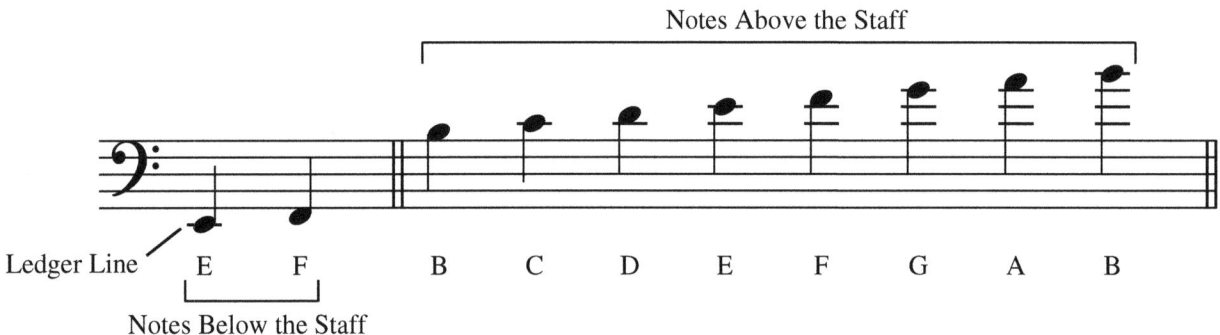

Accidentals: Sharps, Flats, and Naturals

An *accidental* is a symbol that is placed in front of a note to raise or lower its pitch. We'll discuss this topic in greater detail in the next sections of the book, but here are the basics.

Placing a *sharp* (♯) before a note raises it a half step—up one fret on the bass.

Placing a *flat* (♭) before a note lowers it a half step—down one fret on the bass.

Placing a *natural* (♮) before a note restores the note that has been changed by a *sharp* (♯) or *flat* (♭) to its former pitch or fret.
    The key thing to remember when reading music is that when an accidental is written in front of a note, it lasts for the *duration of that measure.*

Key Signature

A *key signature* is the next item placed to the right of the bass clef at the beginning of the staff. The key signature indicates all of the pitches that are to be played sharp (♯) or flat (♭) *throughout the entire piece of music.*

Time Signatures

The *time signature* is the next item to the right of the key signature at the beginning of the staff. The time signature consists of two stacked numbers. The upper figure indicates the number of beats, or counts, in a measure.

4/4 means there are 4 beats in a measure.

3/4 means there are 3 beats in a measure.

The lower figure indicates which kind of note receives a full beat, or count.

4/4 means quarter notes get one beat

6/8 means eighth notes get one beat

The most frequently used time signatures, or *meters*, are 4/4, 3/4, 2/4, 6/8, and 12/8. There also are many other time signatures, such as 2/2, 3/2, 6/4, 5/4, 9/8, etc. Regardless, the top number will always indicate how many beats are in a measure, and the bottom number will indicate the value of the count. For this book, we'll be using only the simpler meters, like 4/4.

Notes and Rests

The second part to reading music is the rhythm. Each note has duration, as well as pitch. Duration is represented by how many *counts* we give a note. The number of counts—or *beats*—that a note receives indicates how long it is to be played. The chart below refers to 4/4 time.

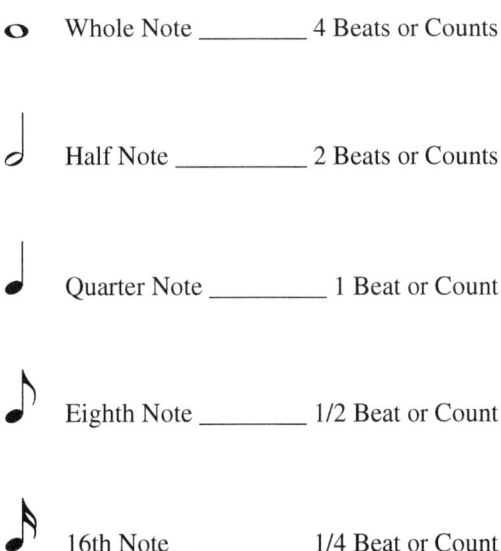

7

A *rest* is the opposite; it tells you how long to be silent—or *rest*—before playing the next note.

𝄻   Whole Rest _____ 4 Beats or Counts

𝄼   Half Rest _____ 2 Beats or Counts

𝄽   Quarter Rest _____ 1 Beat or Count

𝄾   Eighth Rest _____ 1/2 Beat or Count

𝄿   16th Rest _____ 1/4 Beat or Count

Dotted Notes and Ties

A *dot* that is placed immediately after a note increases the note's duration by one-half.

𝅗𝅥. _____ 3 Beats or Counts   =   𝅗𝅥 + 𝅘𝅥

𝅘𝅥. _____ 1 1/2 Beats or Counts   =   𝅘𝅥 + 𝅘𝅥𝅮

𝅘𝅥𝅮. _____ 3/4 Beat or Count   =   𝅘𝅥𝅮 + 𝅘𝅥𝅯

Ties also are used to increase the duration of a note. A tie is an arched line that connects, or "ties," two notes together. Note that the *second tied note does not get struck*.

𝅘𝅥‿𝅗𝅥 = 𝅘𝅥 + 𝅗𝅥   𝅗𝅥‿𝅘𝅥‿𝅘𝅥𝅮 = 𝅗𝅥 + 𝅘𝅥 + 𝅘𝅥𝅮

Ties may connect notes within a measure or between measures.

Tablature

We've included tablature—aka tab—for all of the examples in the book to help you get going. When reading tablature, each tab line represents a different string on your instrument. (The bottom line will always be the lowest string.) Each number placed on a line represents the fret of the string you are supposed to play. A "zero" indicates to play the string *open*—without holding any fret. The following example shows each of the open strings. The sounding pitches of the strings are actually an octave lower than the written pitches.

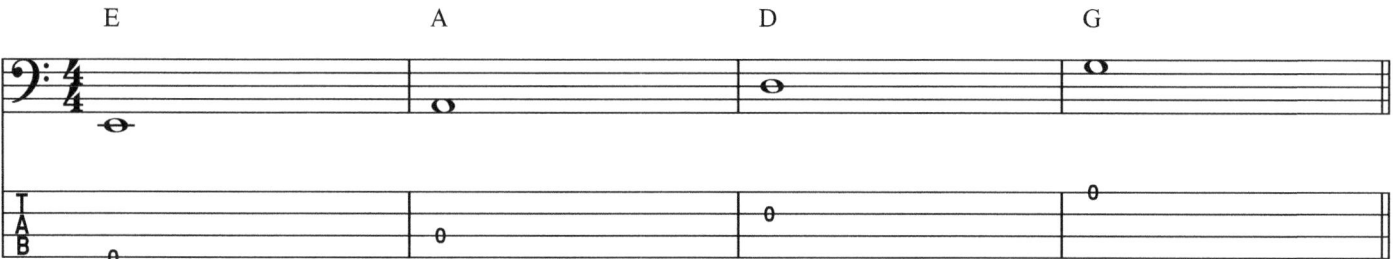

The biggest problem with tab is that it tells you *where* to play but not *when* to play. Take some time to get comfortable with reading music; you'll have a much easier time communicating with other musicians.

Introducing the Bass Guitar

Parts of the Bass

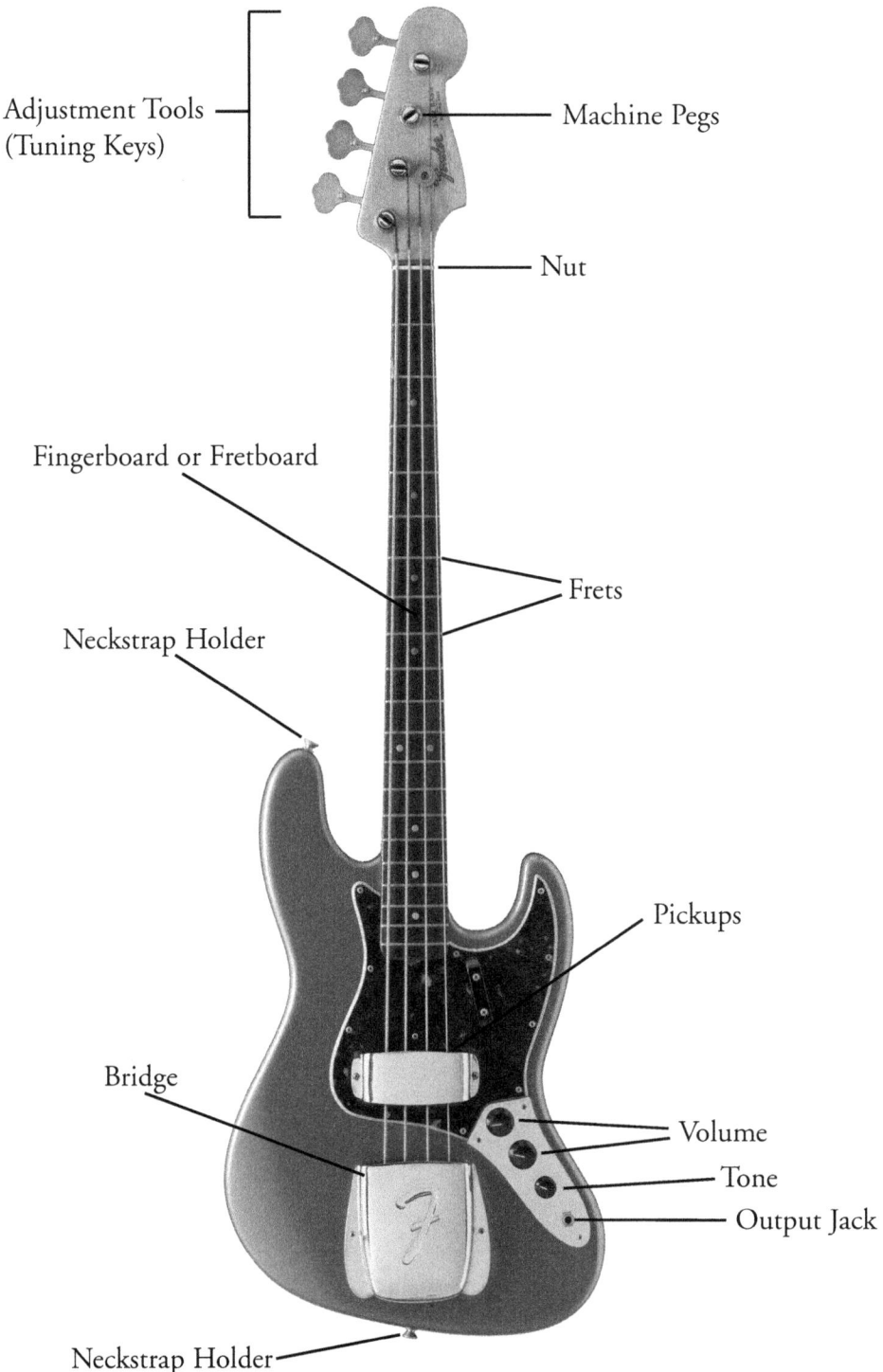

Care of the Bass Guitar and Amplifier

Musical instruments usually are fragile and require careful handling. All string instruments have parts and accessories that are delicately adjusted.

When your bass guitar and amplifier are not in use, they should be kept in a good case or cover and put in a safe place. They must be protected from moisture and changes in temperature. Keep them away from heat sources and cold, drafty places.

If a string breaks, it should be replaced as soon as possible. If you're unable to replace it immediately, loosen the remaining strings to relieve uneven pressure on the neck. It's best to replace your strings before they break, so if they're old, worn, or discolored, replace the whole set.

Clean the neck and fingerboard often to remove oils that are deposited by your fingers. Carry a soft cloth in your case or bag, and clean the instrument after each use. This will prolong the string life, as well.

Some guitar polish applied to the instrument will greatly improve its appearance. Occasionally, the tuning machines may need a drop of light oil.

Tuning the Bass Guitar

There are two basic methods of tuning. You can tune your bass with an electronic tuner or you can tune by ear, using a fixed pitch, like a piano, pitch pipe, or tuning fork.

Electronic Tuners

Today, with the popularity of electronic guitar tuners, tuning has become as simple as plugging in your instrument. Every tuner is a little different, so read that pesky manual that came with your tuner. The greatest advantage of an electronic tuner is the fact that you can precisely tune your bass—even in a loud environment—such as when standing next to that thunderous drummer before a jam session!

While using an electronic tuner is the fastest way to tune, do yourself a favor and occasionally practice tuning by ear. This is the simplest form of ear training!

Tuning by Ear

Tuning to a fixed pitch can be a little difficult to get used to, but everyone can do it with a little practice. The idea is to match the pitch of a string to a known pitch source. Here's what you do:

While the *source pitch* (like a piano or other reference pitch) is playing, strike the appropriate string and let it ring. If the string is out of tune, you will hear a "pulsing" sensation within the two sounds. This pulsing is known as "beats." Let the string vibrate and begin turning the tuner. The beats will get faster and more noticeable as you move *away* from the correct pitch. And, conversely, they'll get slower and calmer as you move *towards* the pitch. Tightening the string will make the pitch higher, and loosening the string will make the pitch lower. (Remember: a small amount of turning may be all that's needed).

Use a piano, tuning track, or other instrument to find these four tones. Begin by tuning the E string (the largest/lowest pitched string) and work across the remaining strings (A, D, and G), tuning each as needed.

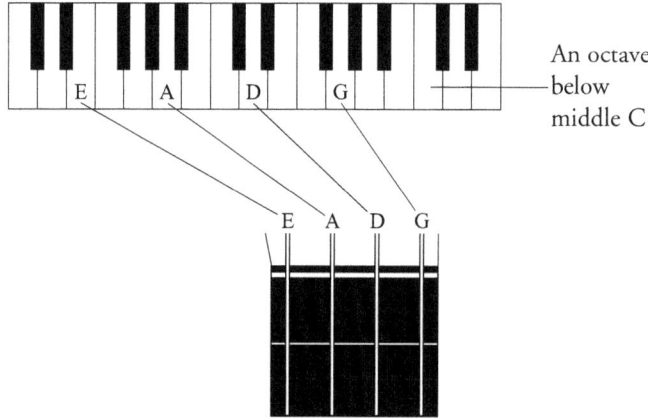

On the companion audio, there is a tuning track that you can use to tune your bass. On the track, you will hear all four strings, from lowest to highest (E–A–D–G), with each string being played three times. Tune each string to match the audio.

 *Tuning Track*

TRACK 01

Many pitch pipes—and all tuning forks—provide only one pitch, which is usually an A. If so, you're not out of luck. You can tune all four strings on the bass from one pitch in this manner:

1. Let's say you have a tuning fork with an "A" pitch. Using the tune-by-ear method describe earlier, adjust your A string until it matches the pitch of the tuning fork.

2. Next, play the 5th fret of the A string and compare it to the pitch of the adjacent open D string. Tune the open D string until it matches the pitch you heard when you struck the 5th fret of the A string.

3. Once you've tuned the A and D strings, move to the G string. Press down the 5th fret of the D string and compare it to the open G string. Adjust the G string until it matches the pitch of the 5th fret on the D string.

4. Now that the top three strings are in tune, move to the E string. Play the 5th fret of the E string and compare it to the open A string. This time, since the A string is in tune and the E string is not, *tune the E string* until it matches the pitch of the open A string.

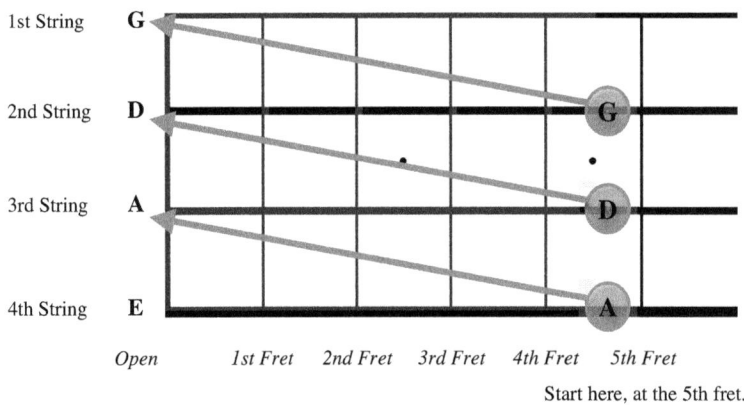

It may seem a bit complicated at first, but after a few tunings, it'll become second nature.

Holding the Bass Guitar

Left Thumb

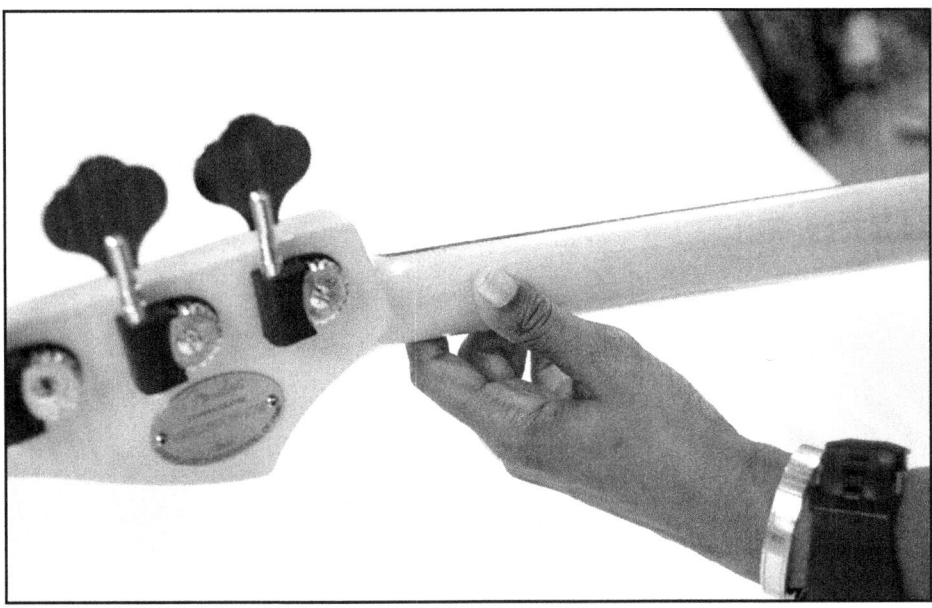

Place the thumb on the neck of the bass guitar, opposite the 2nd (middle) finger. Notice how the fingers are spread open in the palm.

Left Hand

Place the 1st (index) finger behind the 1st fret.
Place the 2nd (middle) finger behind the 2nd fret.
Place the 4th finger (pinky) behind the 3rd fret.
*The 3rd (ring) finger assists the 4th finger (hold the ring and pinky together).

Right Thumb

Rest your thumb on the neck or pickup of the bass. The first two fingers will automatically be in playing position.

Right Hand

The 3rd and 4th fingers should be relaxed (tucked in "handwriting position").

Alternate Right-Hand Position

If you want a brighter sound, play closer to the bridge of the bass. The thumb now will be anchored on the pickup. To gain the most control, your thumb should be anchored somewhere close, along the body of the bass, as shown in the photo.

Standing or Sitting Position

When sitting, do not rest your elbow on your knee. Using a guitar strap will help stabilize the bass. As a starting point, sit and adjust the strap so that the bottom cutout of the bass barely touches your thigh. This will keep the bass at the same height, whether you're sitting or standing.

Attacking the Strings

To attain maximum dexterity, we recommend that you always alternate your 1st and 2nd fingers to attack the strings. It is imperative that your fingernails, on both hands, be clipped short.

Fingerboard Diagram

This diagram shows all of the notes and their locations on the neck of the bass (up to fret 12).

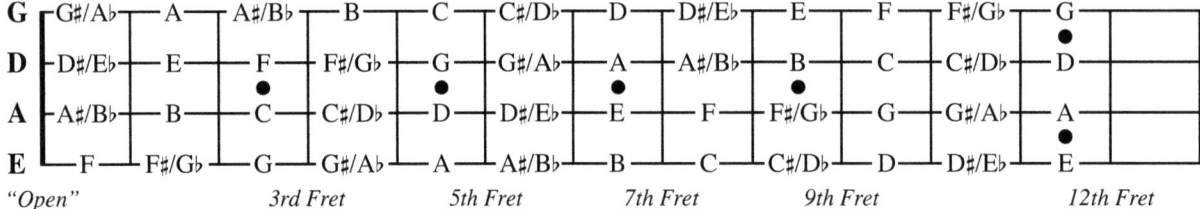

Fingerboard Landmarks

To help you get around the instrument quickly, one of the first things you should do is become familiar with the notes on the neck. I know, I know—it sounds like too much trouble. But it's really easy if you divide the neck into *landmarks* (the marked frets on your bass). First, memorize the open and 12th-fret notes on all of the strings, from low to high (E–A–D–G). They're the same! Then memorize the 3rd (G–C–F–B♭) and 5th frets (A–D–G–C). Finally, memorize the notes at the 7th (B–E–A–D) and 9th frets (C♯–F♯–B–E). You'll soon be able to see a pattern in the layout of notes. Knowing that the 12th fret is the same as the open strings lets you know that every fret thereafter (13th and above) is the same as its corresponding fret 12 frets below (that is, the notes at the 13th fret are the same as those at the 1st fret; the 14th fret is the same as the 2nd, and so on). Easy!

Playing the Open Strings

In this section, we'll begin to play some exercises that use the open strings of the bass. Concentrate on keeping a steady rhythm and getting a good, full sound from the strings. Be sure to pluck only the string that you're aiming for, as accidentally nudging other strings will produce extraneous noise.

Whole Notes

A whole note is played for four counts, or *taps* of your foot. The following examples are played on the open strings so that you can concentrate on counting out loud while tapping your foot. Practice these exercises until you can gracefully alternate the 1st and 2nd fingers of your right hand while playing each note.

At the beginning and the end of each exercise are *repeat signs* (||: :||). When you see repeat signs, play the music between them twice.

Using a Metronome

There is no quicker way to build your ability to read and understand rhythms than by using a metronome. Think of the metronome as someone to help you keep the beat while you count. Each "click" of the metronome will represent a beat in the measure. We suggest that you always tap your foot to develop a strong, consistent rhythmic feel. Be sure to count out each beat as you tap: "1, 2, 3, 4, 1, 2, 3, 4," etc. Start slowly and gradually speed up as your confidence increases.

TRACKS 02-12

TRACK 02

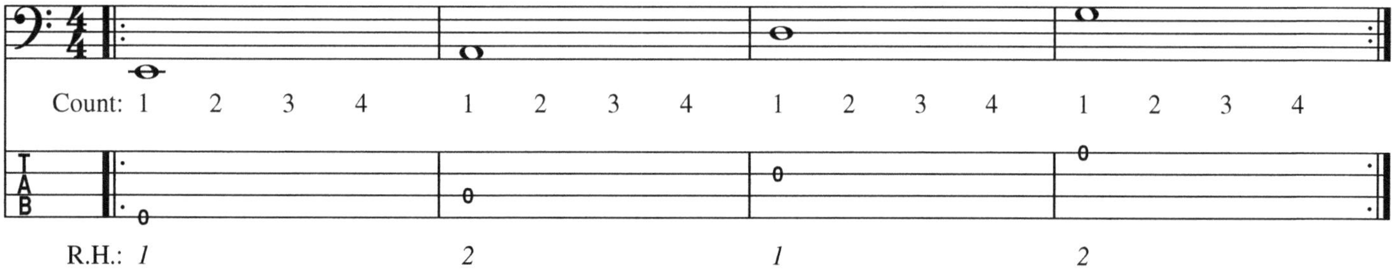

TRACK 03

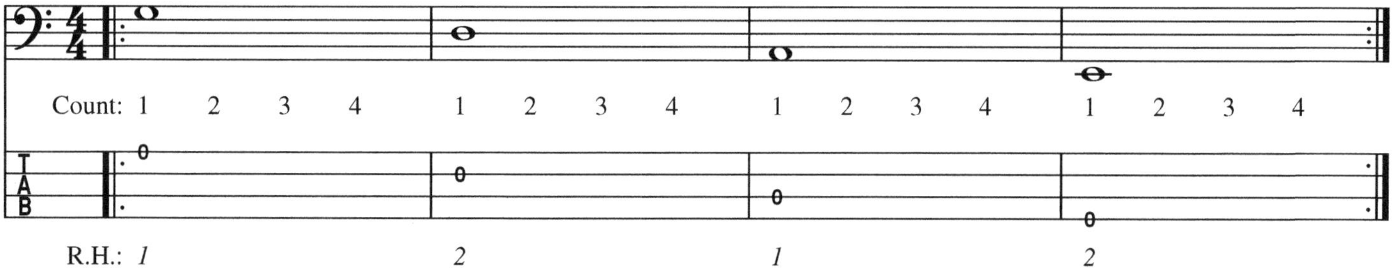

TRACK 04

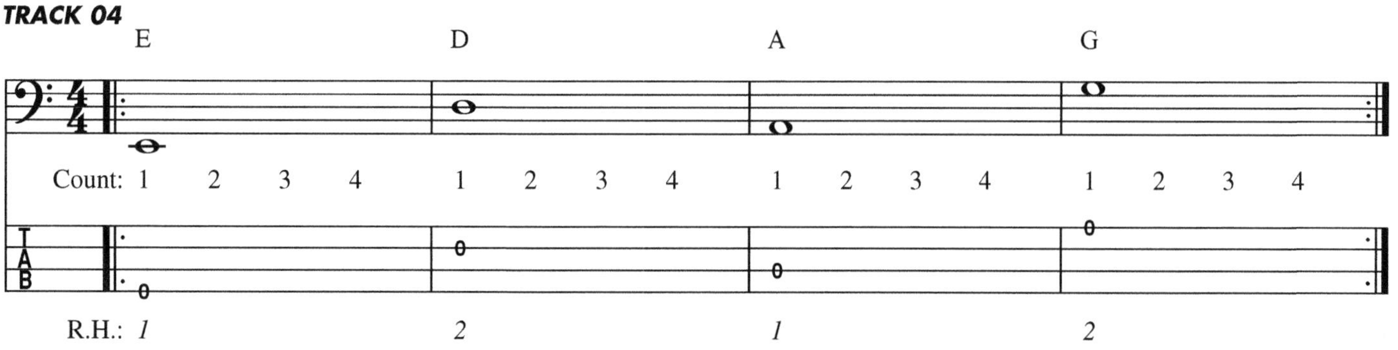

TRACK 05

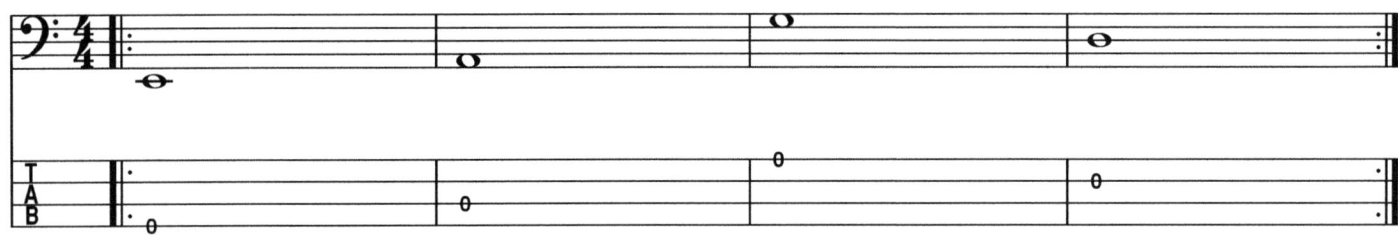

TRACK 06

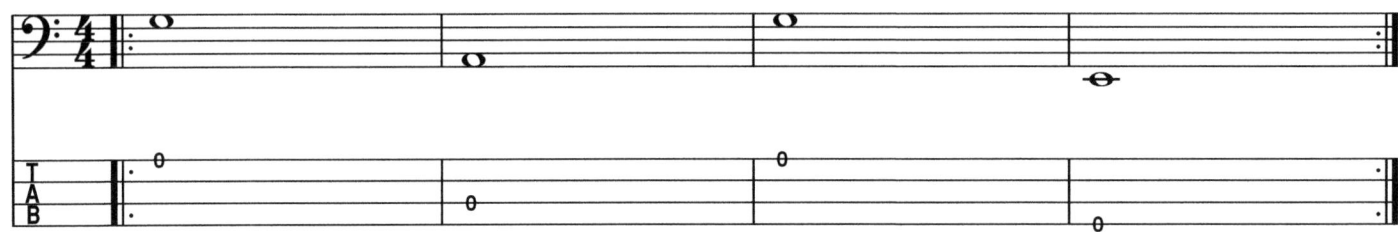

TRACK 07

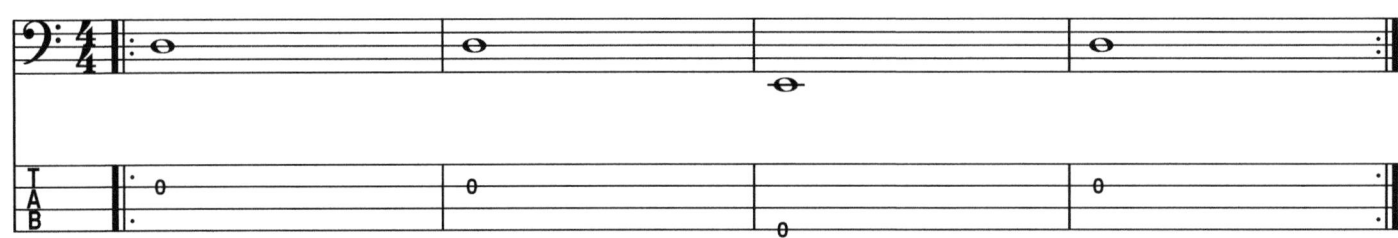

TRACK 08

TRACK 09

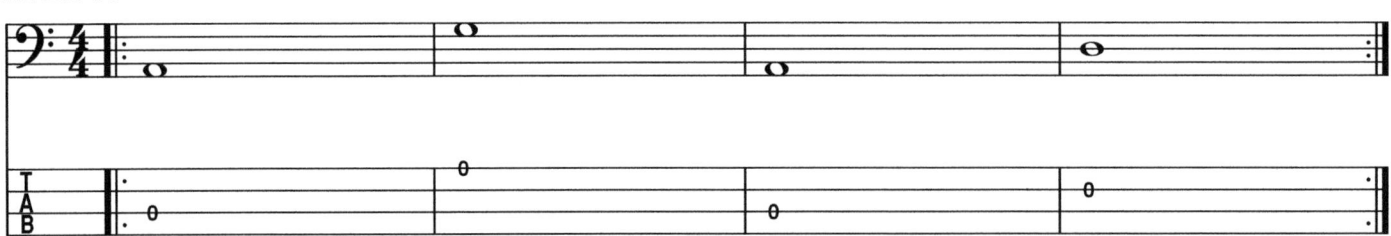

TRACK 10

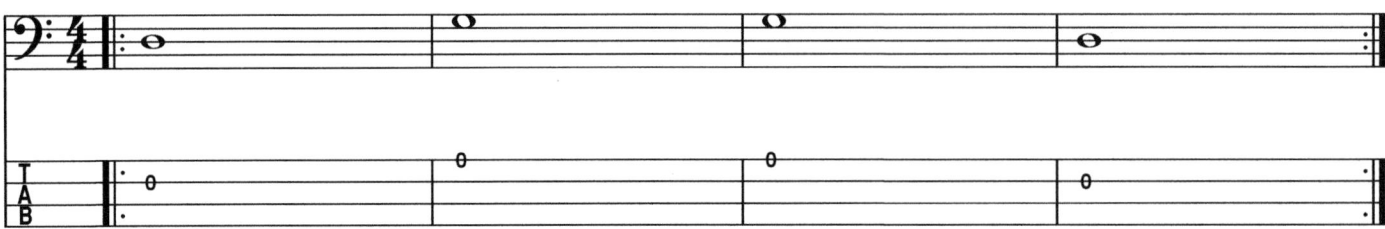

TRACK 11

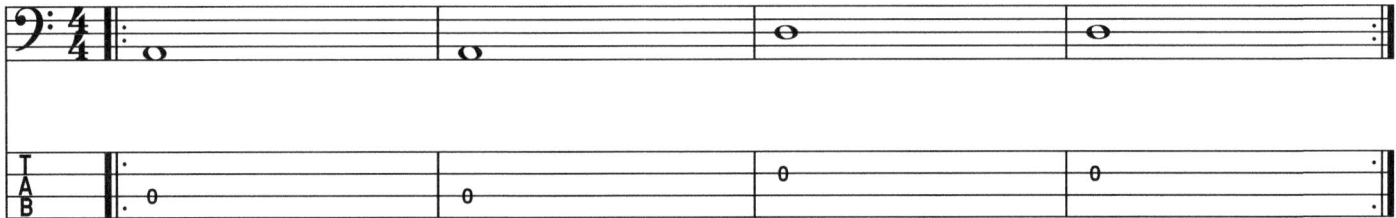

TRACK 12

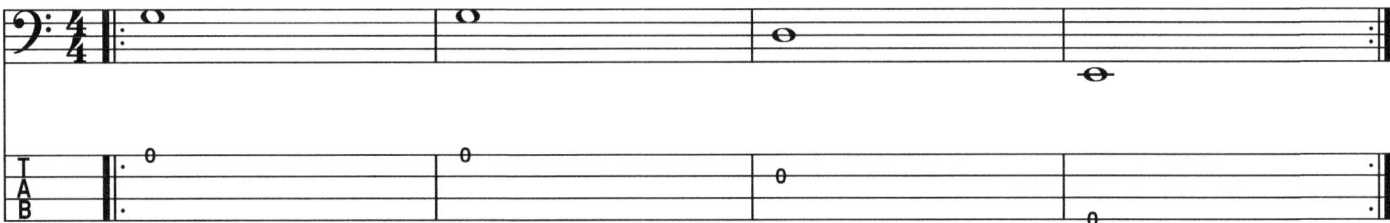

Half Notes

Each half note gets two beats. There are four beats in each measure, so be sure to count "1, 2" for the first half note and "3, 4" for the second half note. Tap your foot while playing each note. Try to *hear* or sing the notes as you are playing them.

TRACK 13

Quarter Notes

Quarter notes are equal to one beat. In this example, there is a mixture of whole, half, and quarter notes. Be sure to consistently *count four beats*—"1, 2, 3, 4"—regardless of the type of note you're playing. Use your metronome and remember to tap your foot.

TRACK 14

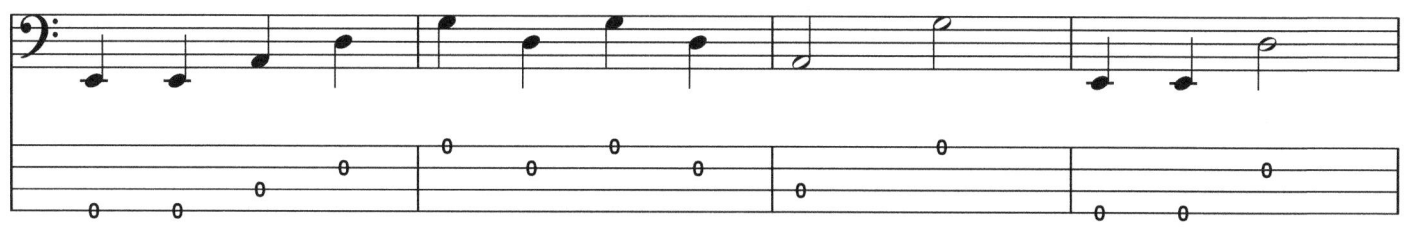
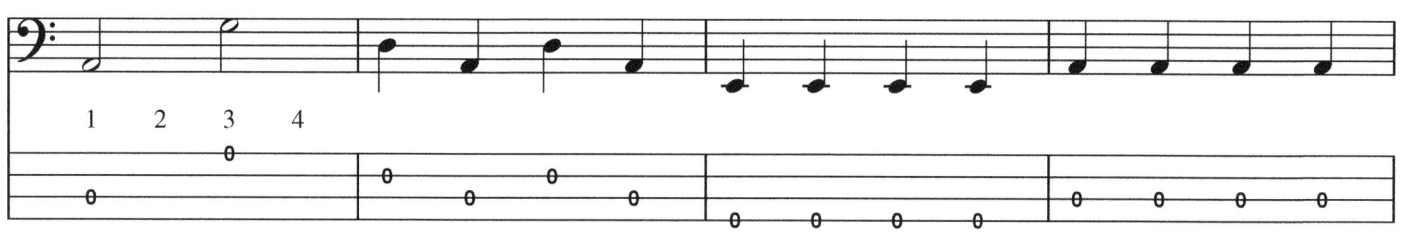
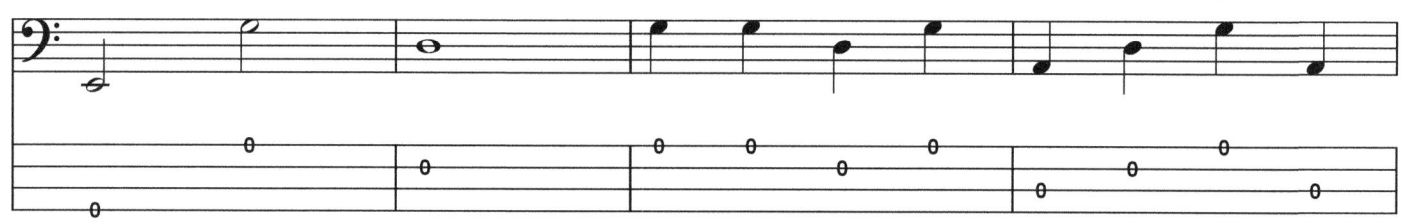
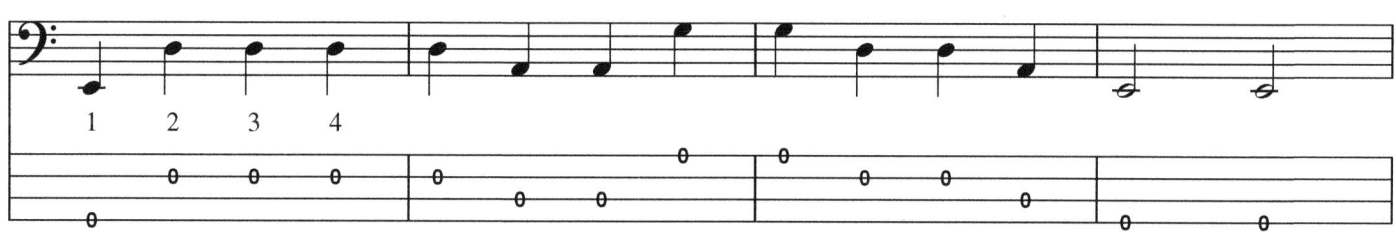
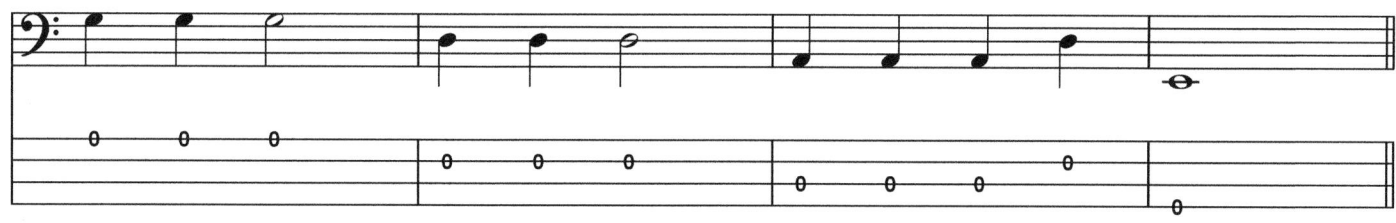

21

Eighth Notes

An eighth note is half of a quarter note. This means that there are two eighth notes in each quarter note, and eight eighth notes in a 4/4 bar.

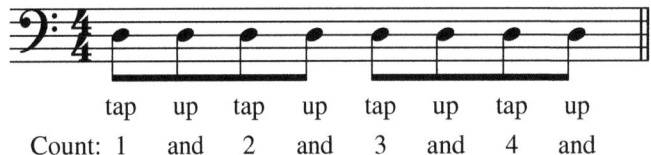

For each tap of your foot, there are two eighth notes. The first eighth note is played when your foot taps the floor; the second eighth note is played when your foot is off the floor. To help simplify things, count out, "1–and, 2–and, 3–and, 4–and." Practice slowly, gradually increasing the speed. If you are having trouble, break the exercise up into four-measure chucks. Master each one separately, and then put them together to play the whole thing.

TRACK 15

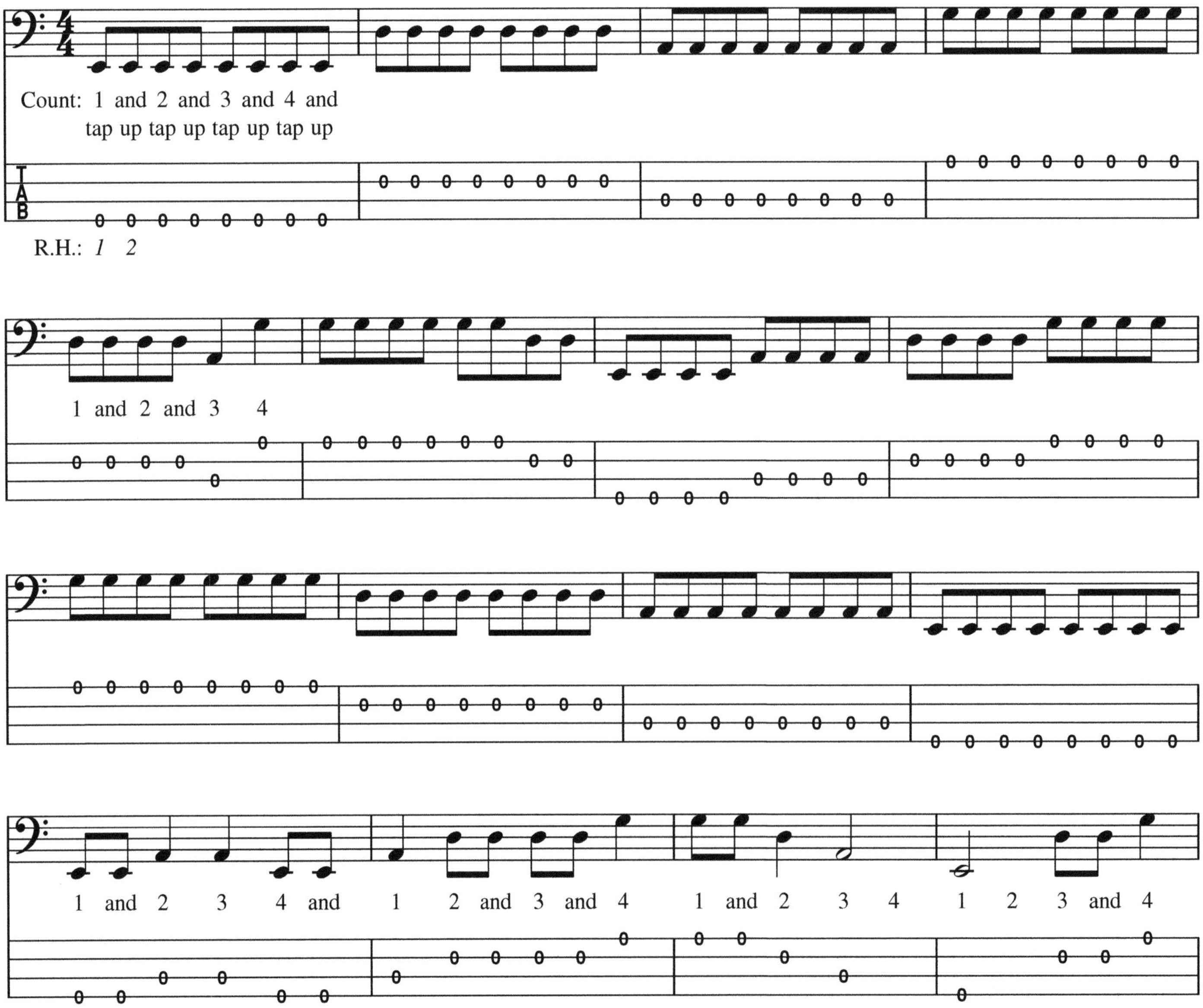

Triplets

A *triplet* is a rhythmic grouping of three equal notes played in the time of two. You can quickly identify triplets by the little "3" that is centered above or below the note grouping.

The figure below shows three eighth-note triplets in place of two eighth notes for each beat. You can verbalize a triplet by saying, "tri–pel–let." Or, if you like, using any three-syllable word would work, like "con–cen–trate" or "sim–pli–fy." Be sure to evenly divide the beat into *three equal parts*. To help keep your place in the measure, try counting the triplets as follows: "1–is–a, 2–is–a, 3–is–a, 4–is–a."

TRACK 16

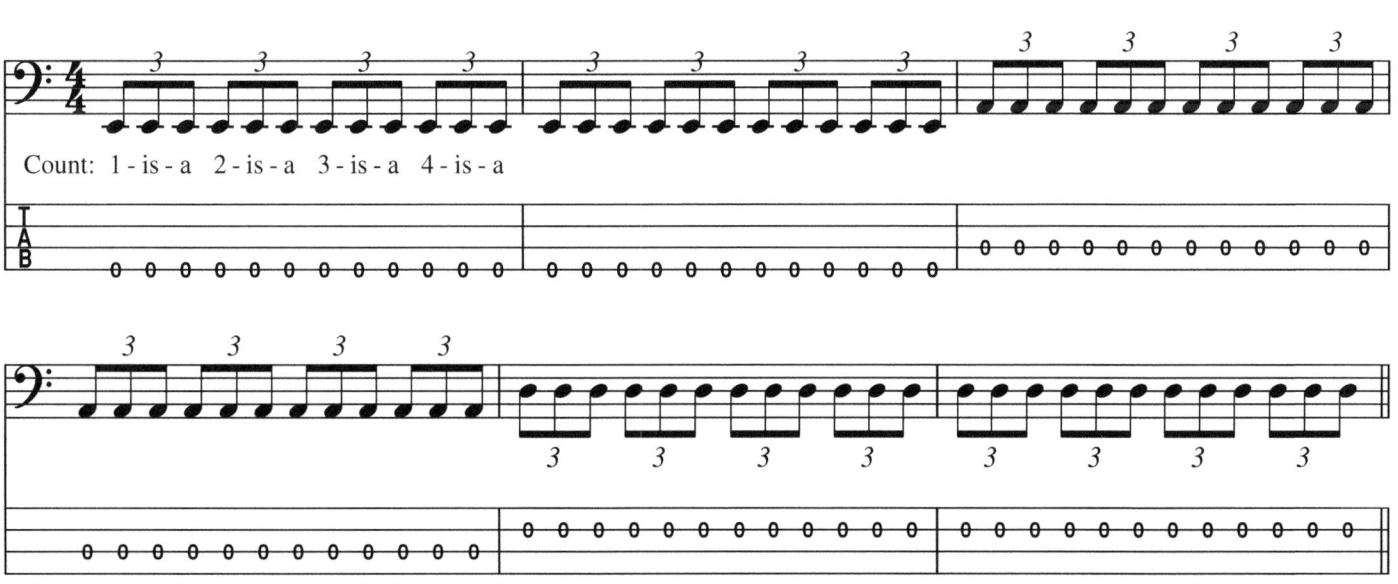

23

The Shuffle Rhythm

While the exact origin of the word "shuffle," in reference to contemporary music, is debatable, the feel has been borrowed and shared across many styles of music but is commonly associated with boogie and blues styles. The rhythm has an exciting feel and is constantly moving. It has the sound and feel of skipping down the street as if you were saying, "skip-ti, skip-ti, skip-ti, skip-ti." To get the feel of the shuffle rhythm, play a triplet, leaving out the middle note, as shown in the example below.

Practice slowly, gradually increasing the speed.

TRACK 17

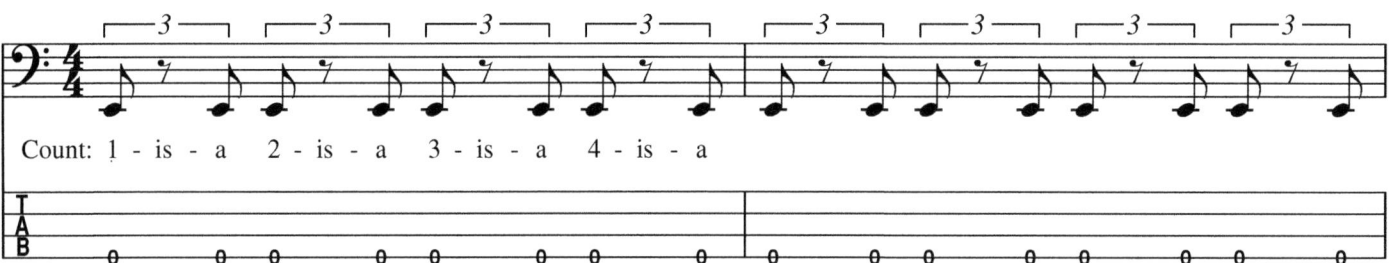

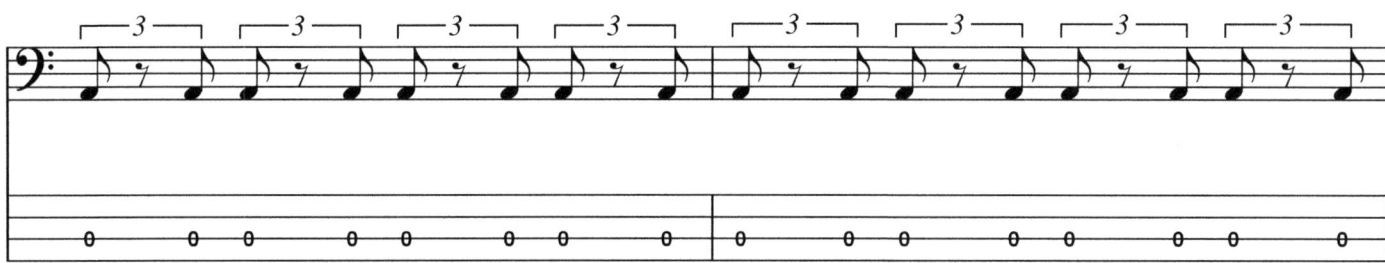

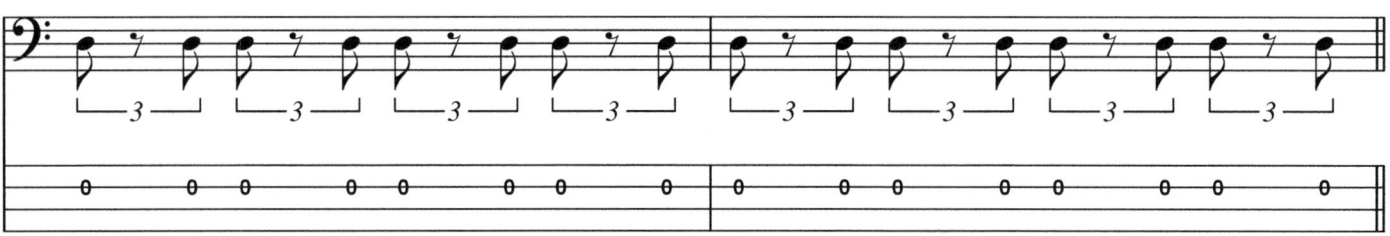

A Variation of the Shuffle Rhythm

This variation uses 16th notes instead of triplets, yet it still has a skipping feel. There are four 16th notes in each quarter note; they're counted "1–e–and–a, 2–e–and–a, 3–e–and–a, 4–e–and–a." To play this feel, give three of those 16th notes to the dotted eighth and one to the sixteenth.

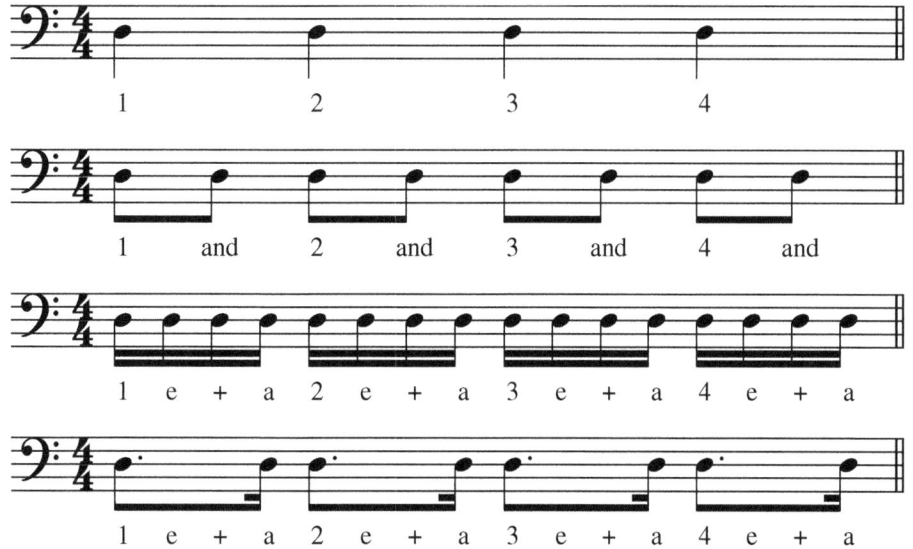

TRACK 18

E Blues Shuffle

The following example is a simple E blues shuffle. Measure 9 will be played on the 2nd fret of the A string. Try to keep a steady rhythm while shifting strings throughout the song.

TRACK 19

Notes on the First Three Frets

Half Steps and Whole Steps

The musical alphabet consists of whole steps and half steps. The distance between every fret on your bass is a *half step*. The distance between every two frets is called a *whole step*; just remember that two halves make a whole.

The musical alphabet uses the following pitches: A–B–C–D–E–F–G. The most important thing to remember is: *there is only a half step (1 fret) from B to C and from E to F*. The distance between all other consecutive pitches is equal to a whole step. You can use your bass to visualize the notes.

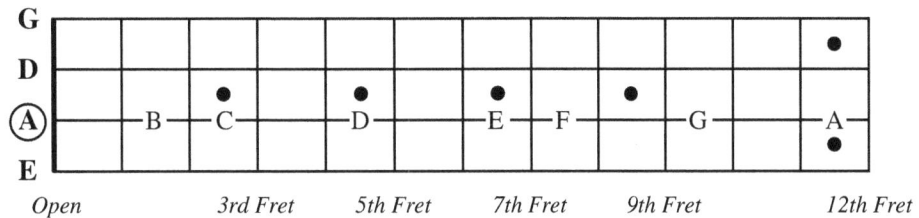

The Chromatic Scale

Notice that there are "gaps" in the musical alphabet on the neck. Filling in these spaces creates the *chromatic scale*, making it a series of 12 equally spaced half-step pitches. Filling in the missing notes is easy—just use a sharp (♯) to raise the pitch or a flat (♭) to lower it. Use your bass to spell the A chromatic scale. Starting with the open A string, say and play each note up the scale/neck. Use sharps for the notes that go up the neck and use flats for the notes that come back down. *Remember, there is no sharp or flat between B and C and between E and F.*

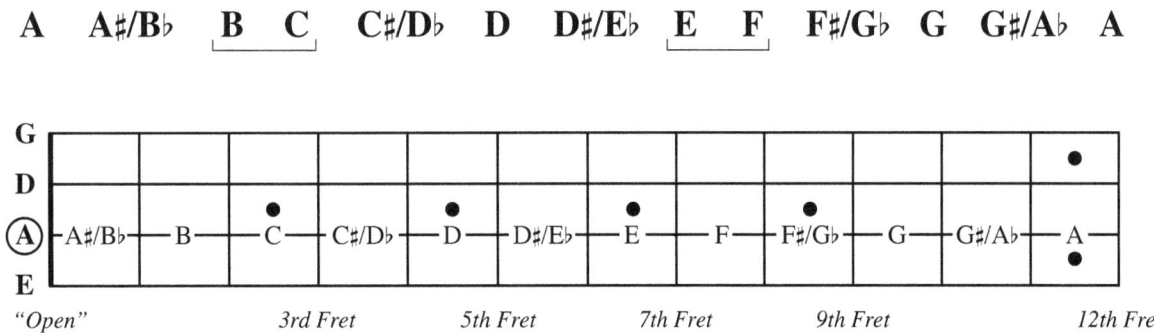

Enharmonic Equivalents

Enharmonic equivalents are notes that sound the same but are written differently. In the previous diagram, we just saw how the note on the 1st fret of the A string can be called either A♯ or B♭. Both are correct! A♯ is the enharmonic equivalent of B♭, and B♭ is the enharmonic equivalent of A♯.

Playing the First Three Frets

When the 1st finger is placed on the fingerboard *behind* the first fret—or away from the bridge—the hand will fall naturally into position to play the first three frets (and half steps) on each string.

During your first attempts to play the following exercise, your hands and fingers may not be strong enough to play with any finesse or ease. Don't become discouraged. You'll need to press down hard enough to keep the string from buzzing under your finger. As you continue to practice, your hand will strengthen and the results will be gratifying.

The numbers placed under the notes on the staff are used to illustrate the proper fretting finger.

0 = open: play the string "open," without any fingers holding any frets.
1 = index finger
2 = middle finger
3 = ring finger
4 = pinky

Don't confuse these numbers with the numbers used on the tab staff. The numbers on the tab staff represent a fret to be played on any given string; these numbers indicate which finger is to be used.

Notes on the G String

The figure below illustrates the names of the notes, their enharmonic equivalents (if any), where they are located on the staff, as well as the proper fingering.

When playing with your 2nd finger, be sure to *keep your 1st finger down to help hold the string*. Even more so, when playing with your 4th finger, be sure to use *all of your fingers* to help hold down the string. This will be a tough challenge for a lot of beginners. Just keep at it!

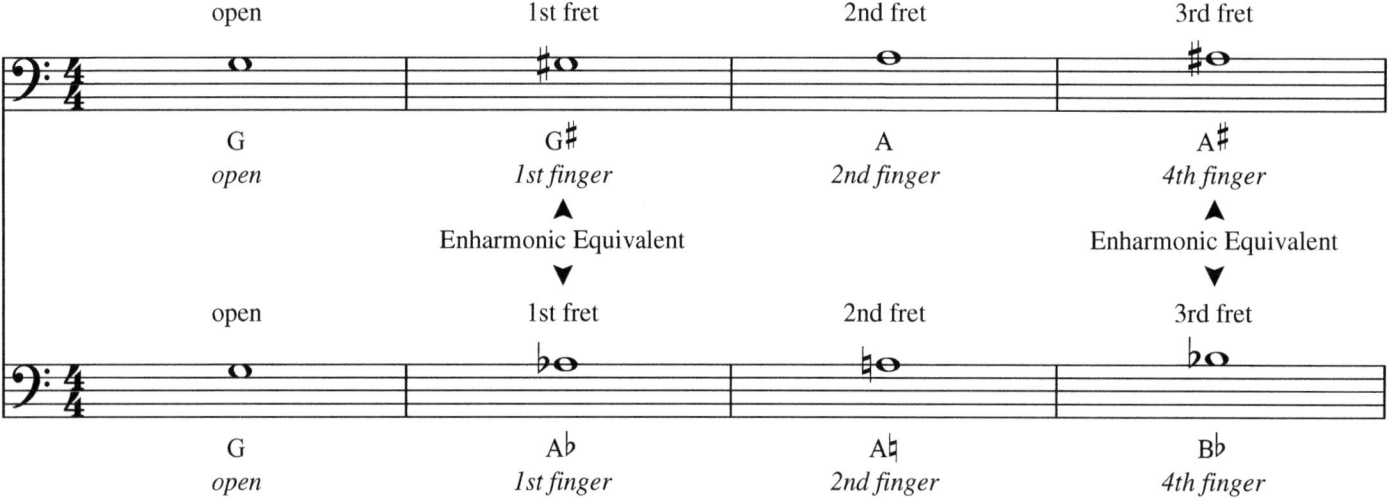

Exercise – G String

TRACK 20

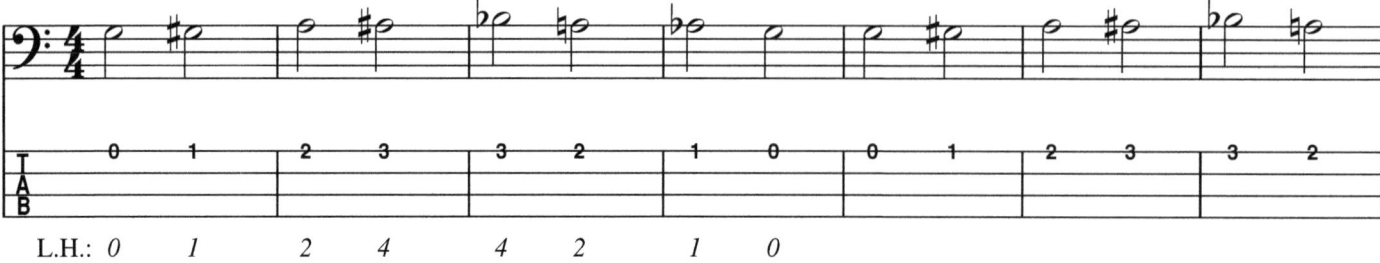

Notes on the D String

Even though there is only a half step from B to C and E to F, these notes also have enharmonic equivalents. On the D string, when E is raised a half step (or one fret), the E becomes E♯. Enharmonically, E♯ is the same as F♮. Conversely, when F is lowered a half step (or one fret), it becomes F♭. Enharmonically, F♭ is the same as E♮.

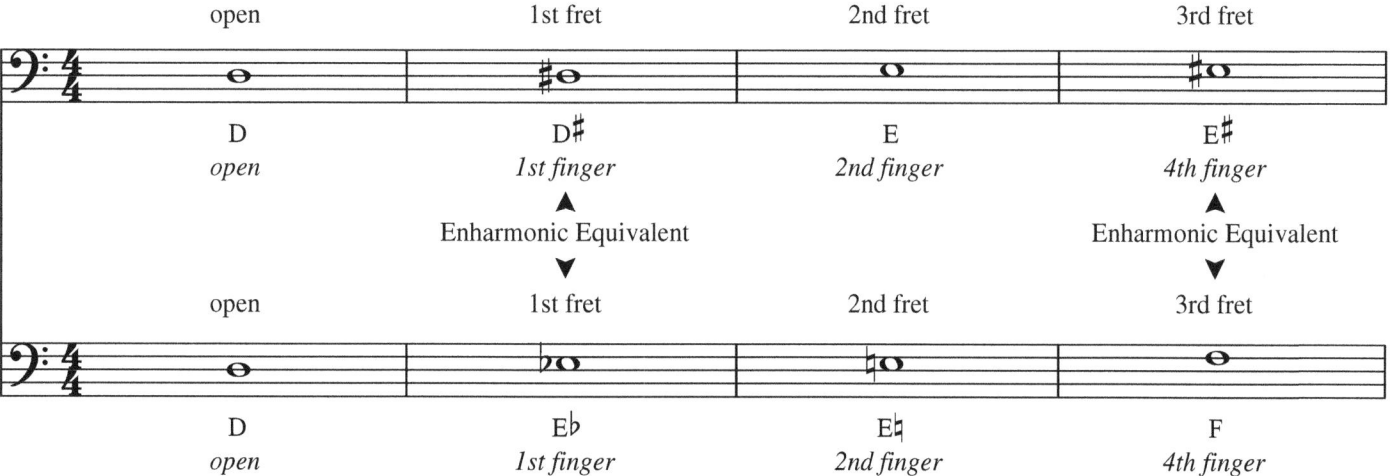

Exercise – D String

TRACK 21

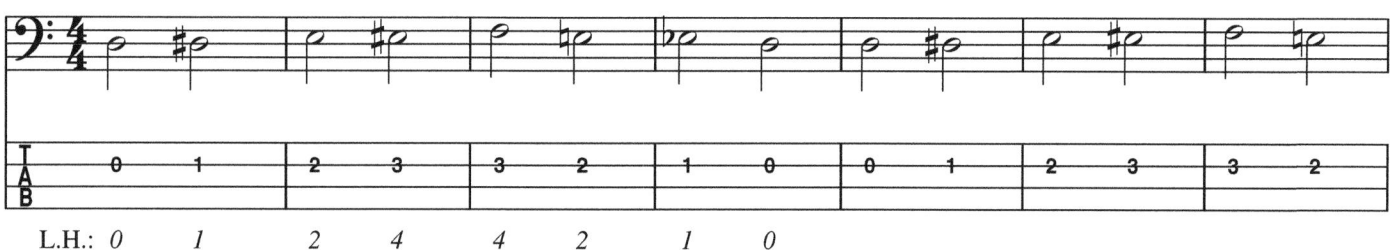

Notes on the A String

The same enharmonic principle applies to B and C on the A string.

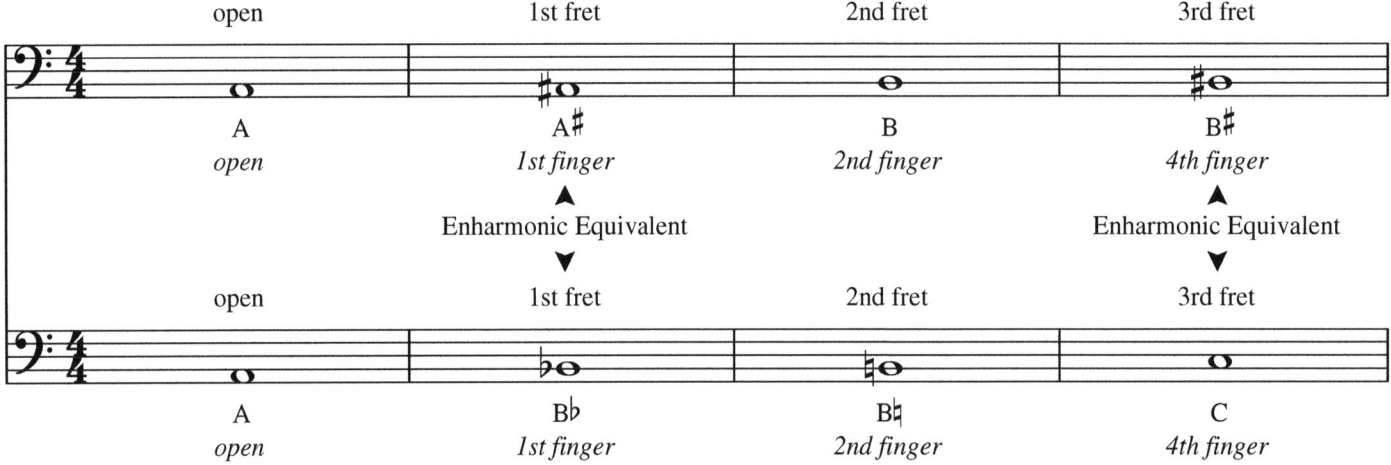

Exercise – A String

TRACK 22

Notes on the E String

The same enharmonic principle applies to E and F on the E string.

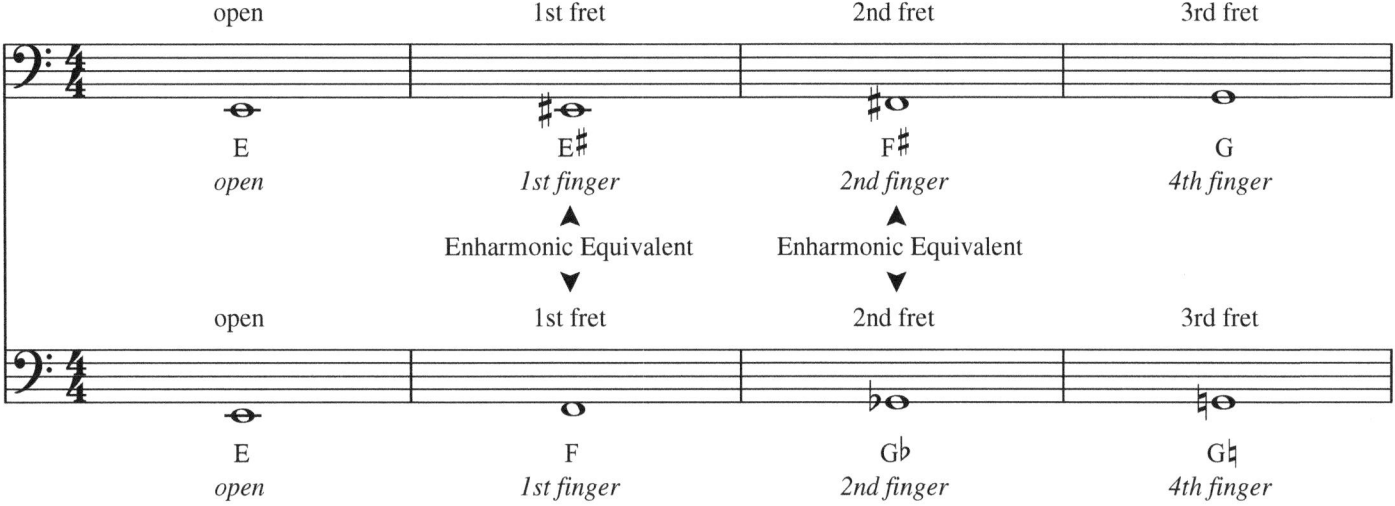

Exercise – E String

TRACK 23

Connecting All Four Strings

Practice slowly at first.

TRACK 24

TRACK 25

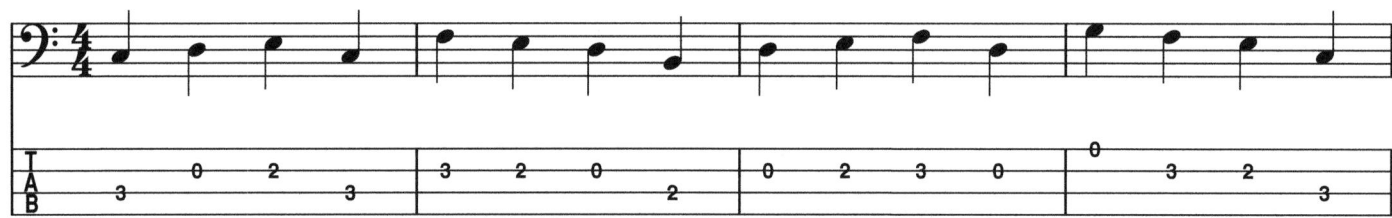

"Jingle Bells"

Using the same notes, play the song "Jingle Bells."

TRACK 26

These next two examples incorporate some more accidentals (sharps and flats), so take your time to make sure you're getting the notes right.

TRACK 27

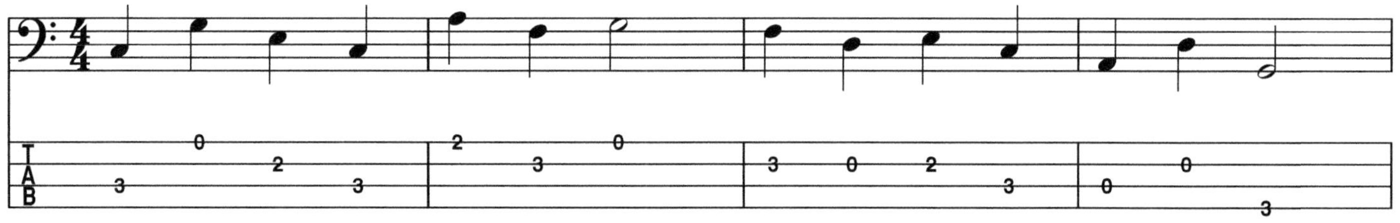

In this example, a *courtesy accidental* is used in the sixth measure, on the note B. Even though the flat symbol (♭) that precedes the B in measure 5 is technically only active until the end of that measure, it's common to use a courtesy accidental in the subsequent measure to remind the performer of the key signature.

TRACK 28

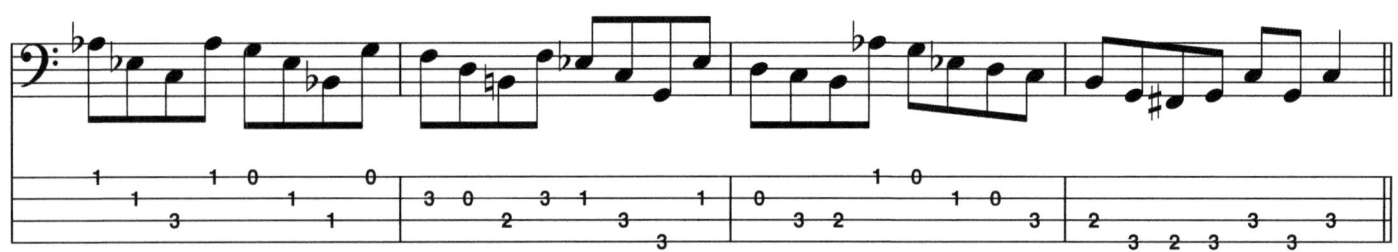

34

Slappin' Basics

The following exercises teach a completely different right-hand technique on the bass guitar. The side of your thumb is actually used to *thump*, or *slap*, the string as though you were striking it with a drumstick.

Your understanding of this technique, along with other techniques in this book, will be enhanced with the amount of time you practice every day. Remember, whatever you do most of your time is what you do best. We suggest that you practice the following exercise and constantly observe the photos below, with regard to the correct position of the thumb and fingers, until a graceful command has been achieved.

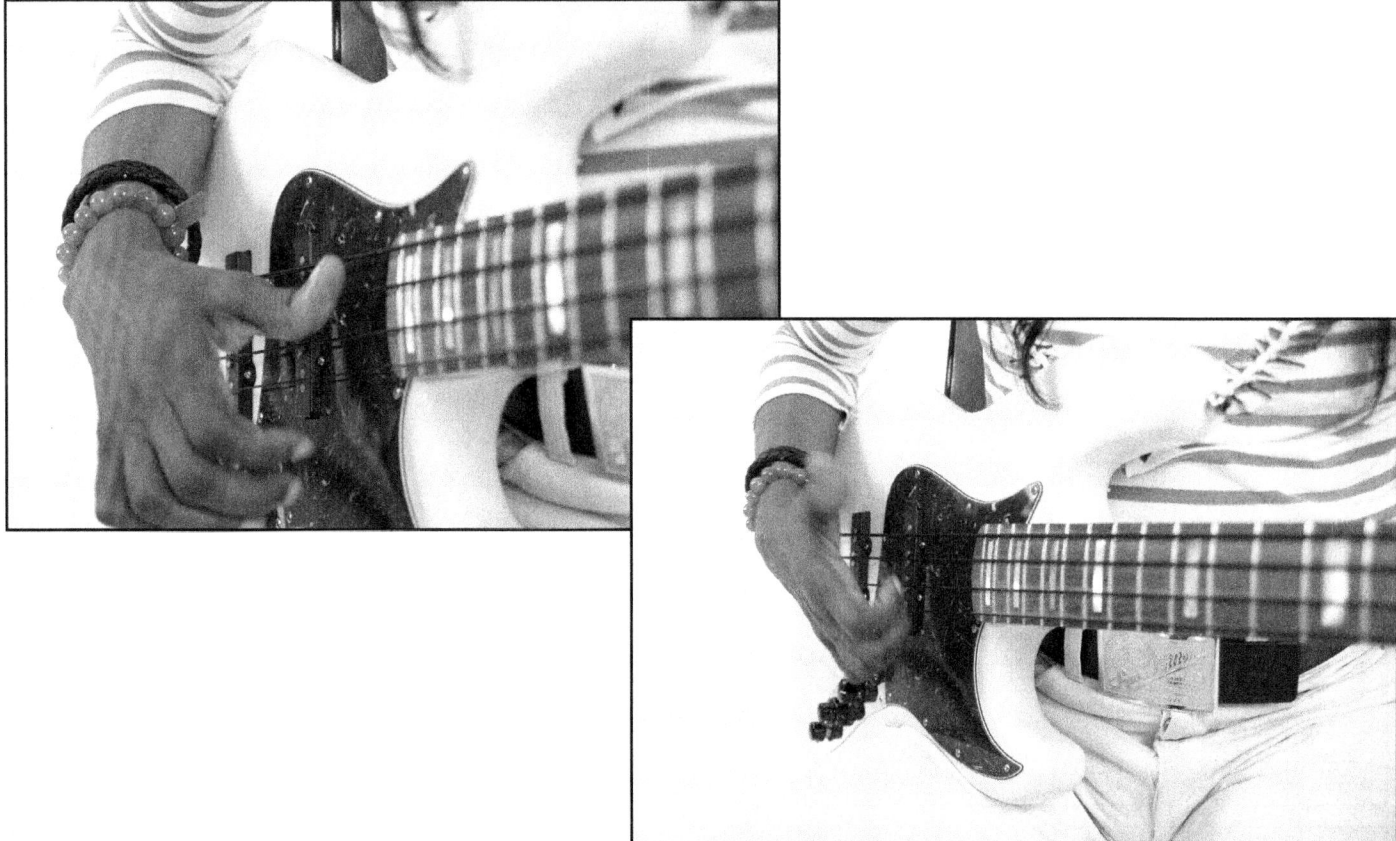

Playing (Thumping) with the Thumb on the E and A Strings

The idea is to use the side of your thumb (at the first knuckle) like a drumstick to strike the string into the fingerboard. It helps to make use of the frets at the upper end of the fingerboard to create that distinctive percussive "slap!" The key is to hit the string *into the fretboard* and let it bounce off of the frets. Don't let your thumb rest on the string. While playing this exercise, pay close attention to the tone of each note as you thump.

In measures 14, 16, and thereafter, you'll see a *one-bar repeat sign* (⁄.). This symbol tells you to repeat the material from the previous measure. Be sure that you keep counting and moving forward through the music!

In the last measure, beats 1 and 2 are *picked* with the index finger of your right hand instead of your thumb. Use the index and middle fingers (held together) to gently pluck the string in an upward motion. Be careful—don't pull the string too hard!

TRACK 29

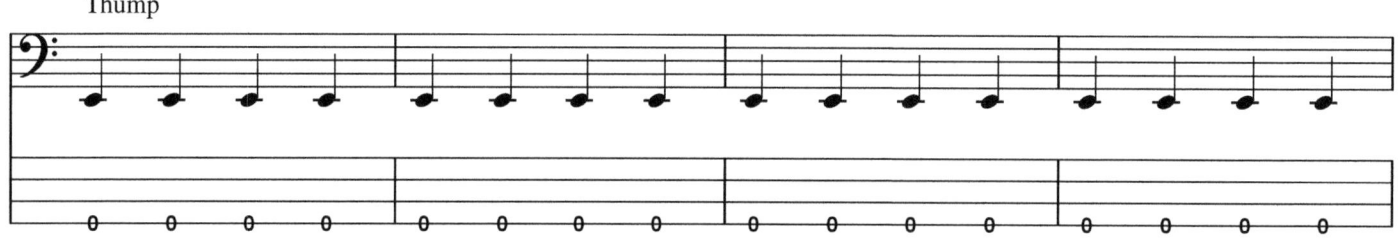

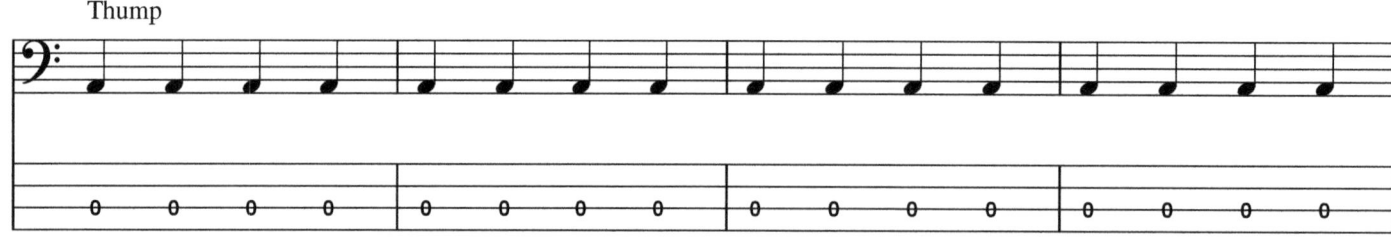

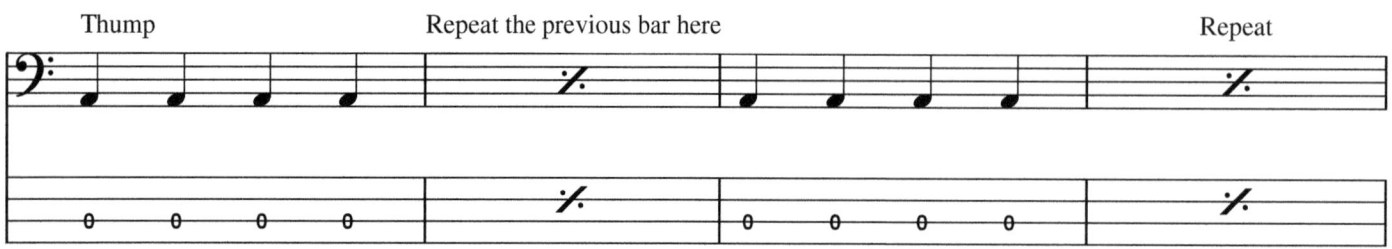

Developing the Thumb-Thumping and Finger-Picking Technique

While you *can* thump on all four strings, it's easier, faster, and more dynamic to combine thumping with a second technique called *picking*, or *popping*. You'll notice that, as you thump a string, your index and middle fingers are *automatically in place to pick the upper strings,* so all you need to do is pick the next note with your index finger. To start, it's best *not to lift* your arm away from the bass but merely *twist your forearm* so that your thumb rises up and down. Notice that, while you twist your forearm, the picking fingers also rotate up!

Alternate thumping the low strings (E and A) with the thumb and picking the high strings (D and G) with the index/middle fingers. The dexterity and flexibility of your right hand will develop only if you practice diligently the following thumb- and finger-strengthening exercises. Practice slowly at first, gradually increasing the tempo. In order to execute this perfectly, pay close attention to the time and rhythm. Playing too rapidly, initially, will give you a muddy sound. Precision and regularity are the real foundation for perfect execution in music.

TRACK 30

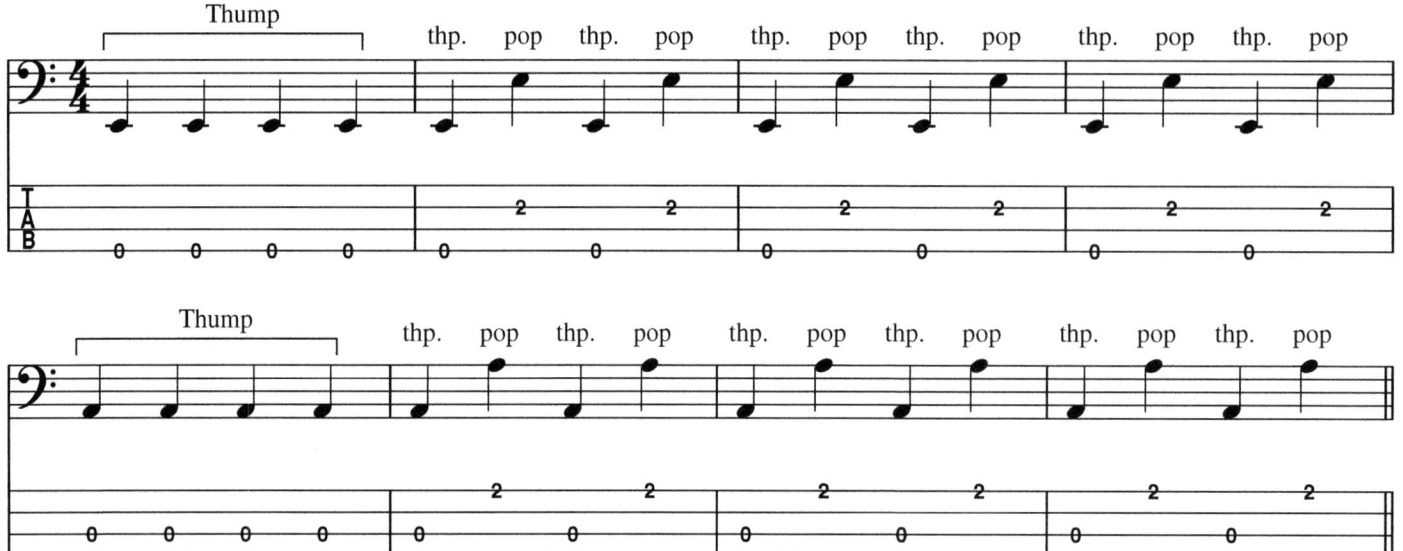

TRACK 31

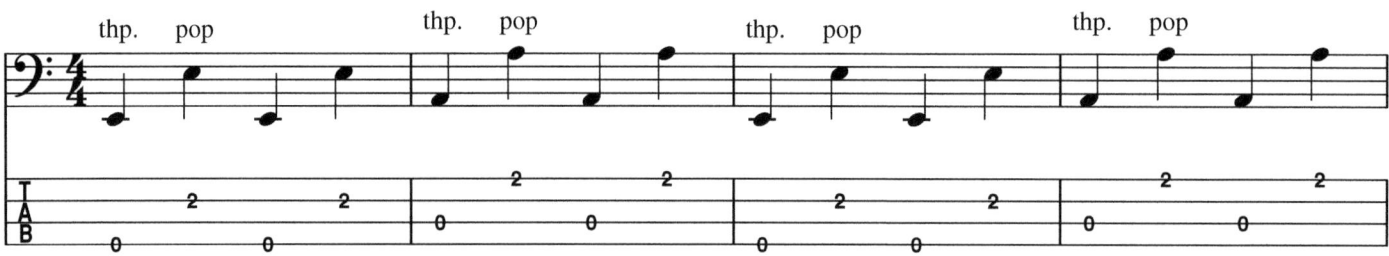

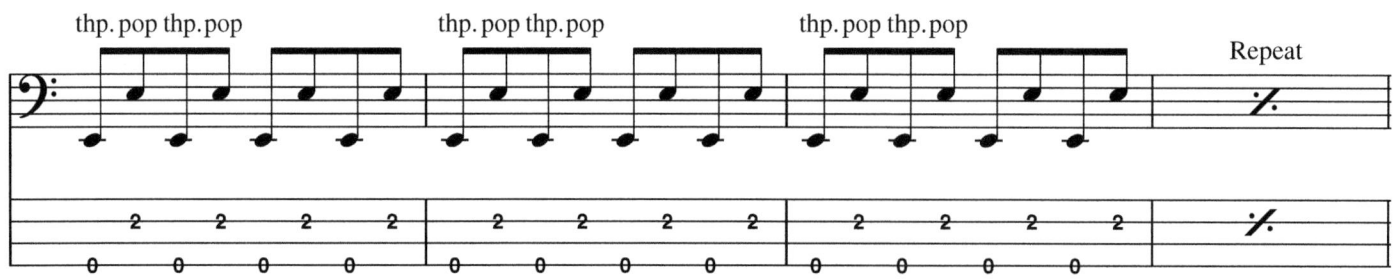

In measures 3–4 and thereafter, you see a *two-bar repeat signs* (𝄎). This symbol simply means that you are to play the same material from the previous two measures. Keep counting and always move forward through the music!

At the end of the following exercise, there is a *hammer-on*. In a hammer-on you play a note and "hammer" down another finger to fret a higher note on the same string *without re-attacking the string*. The easiest way to practice the feel of a hammer-on is to use the open string. Play the open D string and, while the note is ringing, hammer your 1st finger down on the E (2nd fret). Try playing hammer-ons on all of the strings as quarter notes, eighth notes, and 16th notes.

At the end of measure 11, there is a D-string hammer-on. Pick the open D string and quickly hammer on your 2nd finger to play the E (2nd fret). Hold the E note on the D string while quickly jumping back down to thump the open E string. Be sure to let *both* notes ring out for four beats!

TRACK 32

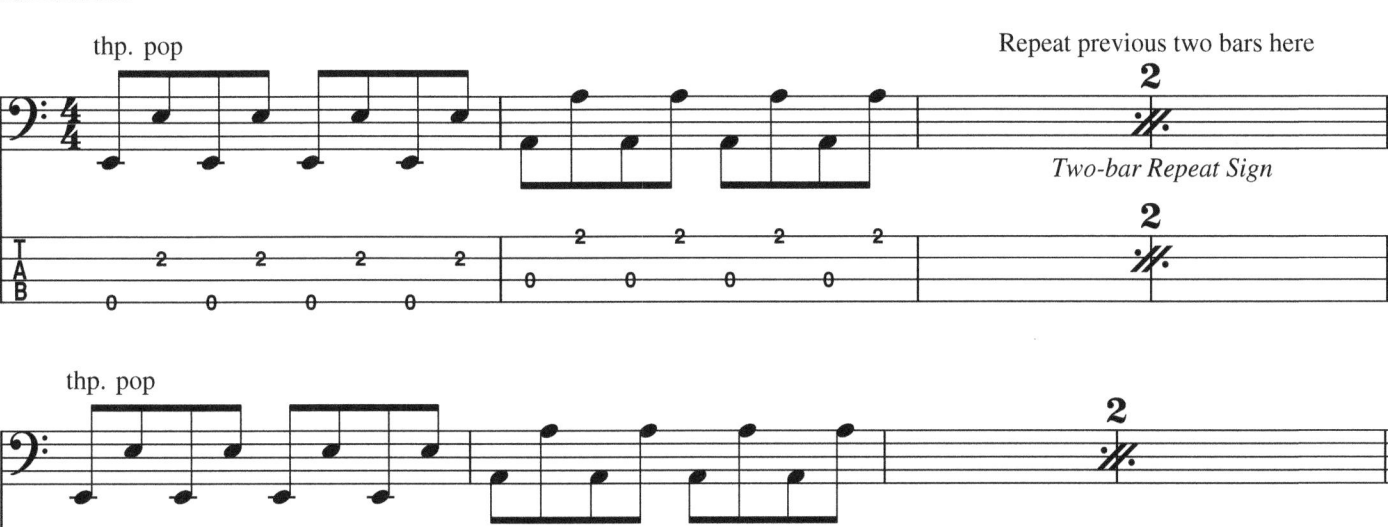

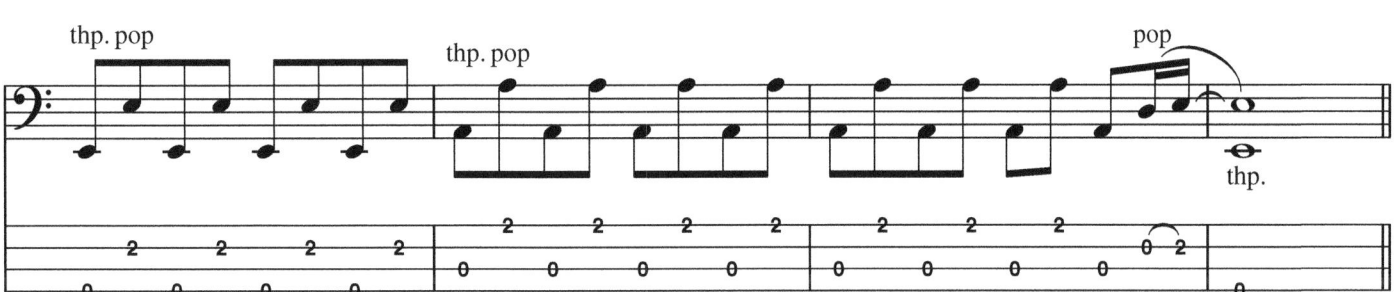

Construction of Major Scales

There are seven natural notes in music—they are the musical alphabet (A–B–C–D–E–F–G). If we start and end on C (C–D–E–F–G–A–B–C), with the last C being one *octave* (eight tones) higher than the first note, these tones create a *scale*—a consecutive series of notes within an octave. This is the C major scale. While there are several kinds of scales, the major scale is, by far, the most common. Major scales are sung to the syllables "Do, re, mi, fa, sol, la, ti, do," or, in descending order, "Do, ti, la, sol, fa, mi, re, do." You may have heard the "Do Re Mi" song from the movie *The Sound of Music*, which illustrates this.

Each note in a scale is assigned a number. The relationship between any two notes in a scale is described by that number and is called an *interval*. In the C major scale, G is an interval of a 5th above C; F is a 4th above C.

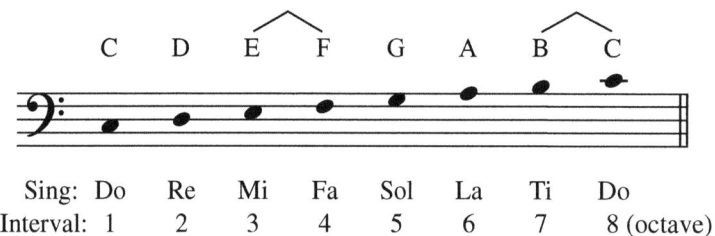

Play E to F on the D string. Notice that there is only one fret between the two notes. Now play B to C on the A string. Again, notice that there is only one fret between the two notes. The distance from E to F and from B to C is called a *half step* because there is no pitch in between the notes. With all other adjacent tones in the C major scale (i.e., C–D, D–E, F–G, G–A, A–B), there are two frets between the notes. As explained on page 27, these are called *whole steps*. All major scales use the same intervallic construction and are formed like this:

1st note to 2nd note = whole step (2 frets)
2nd note to 3rd note = whole step (2 frets)
3rd note to 4th note = half step (1 fret)
4th note to 5th note = whole step (2 frets)
5th note to 6th note = whole step (2 frets)
6th note to 7th note = whole step (2 frets)
7th note to 8th note = half step (1 fret)

Learn to sing this scale with the syllables—"do, re, mi," etc. This will sharpen your ear, especially for discerning half and whole steps, and even improve your singing.

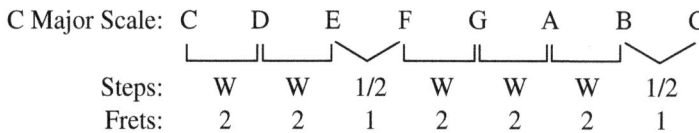

Using the same pattern of whole steps and half steps, we can create all of the major scales—only the C major scale is constructed from all natural tones. The following major scales (G, D, A, E, B, and F♯) must use a sharp (♯) before one or more notes to create the same intervallic pattern. Notice that each scale progressively adds a sharp to the scale *but the sequence of whole and half steps never changes.*

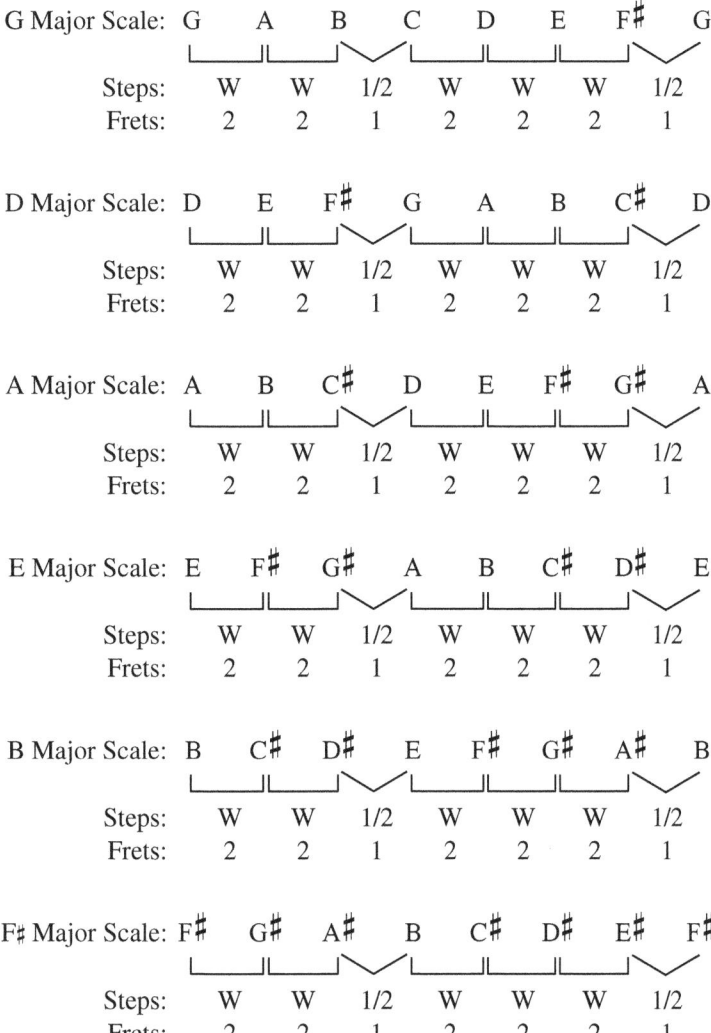

The remaining major scales (F, B♭, E♭, A♭, D♭, and G♭) require the use of a flat before one or more notes to follow the same pattern of half steps and whole steps. Again, each scale progressively adds a flat to the scale.

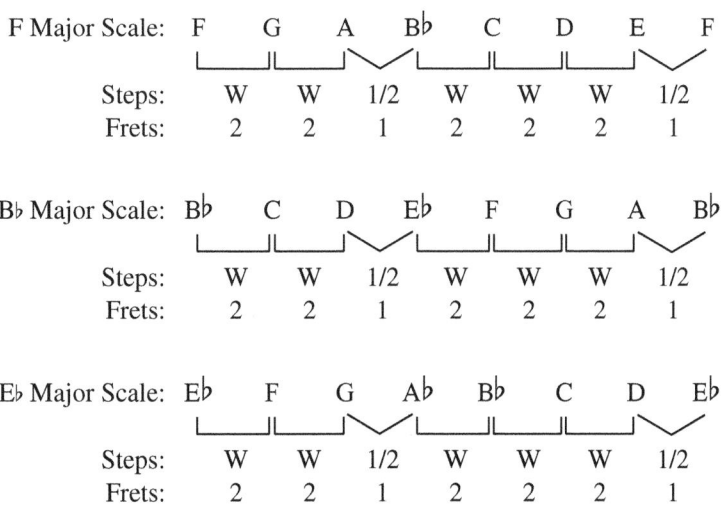

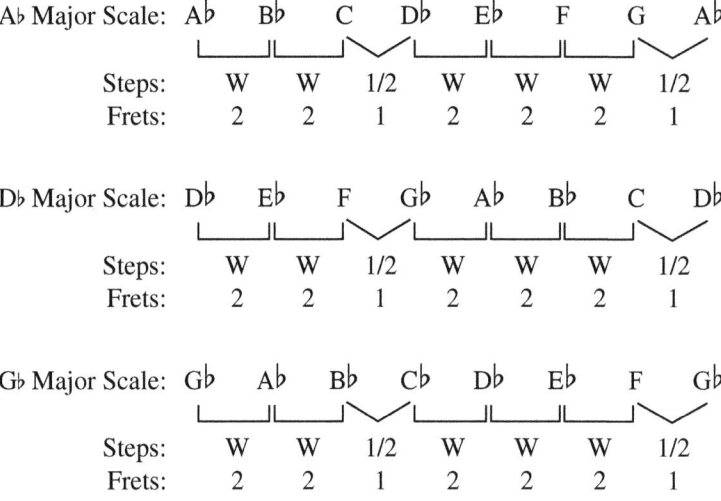

As you move through this book—and up the neck—you'll examine different major scales in each position.

Key Signatures

As explained in the "Rudiments of Music" chapter, it is customary to place sharps and flats at the beginning of each line of music in the form of a *key signature*. Every note indicated with a sharp or flat in the key signature is to be played accordingly throughout the piece of music, regardless of register.

Sharp Keys

The name of the key—and the starting note of a major scale—is called the *key-note*, or *tonic*. The key-note is found a *half step above the last sharp* (farthest to the right) of the key signature. Look at the key of D below. The last sharp in the key signature is C♯, which makes D the key-note—because D is a half step (or one fret) above C♯. The sharps always are placed in a key signature in the same progressive order, from left to right: F♯, C♯, G♯, D♯, A♯, E♯.

Flat Keys

As with keys requiring sharps, flats also are placed in a key signature. The key-note of a flat key is the *next-to-last flat* (to the right) in the key signature. Look at the key of D♭ below. The next-to-last flat in the key signature is D♭, which makes D♭ the key-note. (This system won't work for the key of F, since there's only one flat, so you'll just need to remember that a key signature of one flat indicates the key of F.) The flats always are placed in a key signature in the same progressive order, from left to right: B♭, E♭, A♭, D♭, G♭, C♭.

Accidentals and Naturals

If a sharp or flat is written in any measure without being shown in the key signature, it is called an *accidental*. A particular accidental applies only for the bar in which it is written.

In the key of C, for example, there is no D♯, so an accidental is placed in the music. It will only last for the duration of that measure. A courtesy accidental (in this case, a natural sign) is placed before the D in the following measure, reminding the performer of the key signature. Technically, this is unnecessary, but it is a common "courtesy"!

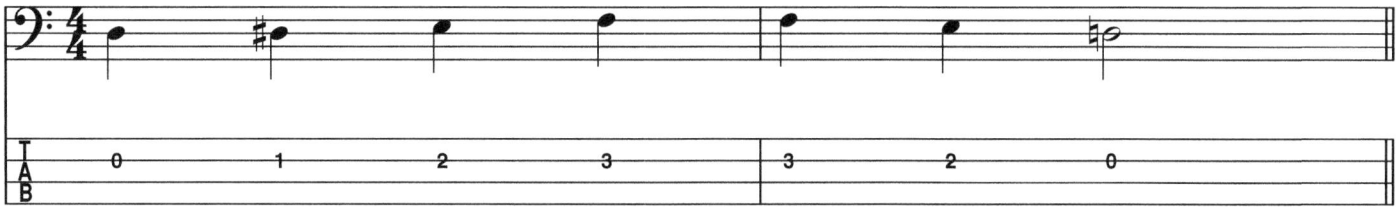

If an accidental is to be cancelled within the same bar, then a natural sign (♮) will be placed before the note to change it back. The natural sign will last the duration of the measure. Notice that beat 3 of the 2nd measure is a D♯ because the previous D♯ lasts for the entire measure. Beat 4, however, is not sharp, as a natural sign cancels it out.

If a note is designated sharp or flat by the key signature, it can also be played as a natural by placing a natural sign before that note.

In the key of G, for example, there is one sharp (F♯). When a natural sign (♮) is placed in the music, it, too, will last only for the duration of that measure (or until another accidental is placed in front of that F note in the same measure).

F Major Scale

In the key of F, there is one flat (B♭), as shown by the key signature. Play the F major scale (F–G–A–B♭–C–D–E–F), ascending and descending. Practice slowly with a metronome, gradually increasing the speed. Try playing the scale up and down as whole notes, half notes, quarter notes, and eighth notes without stopping!

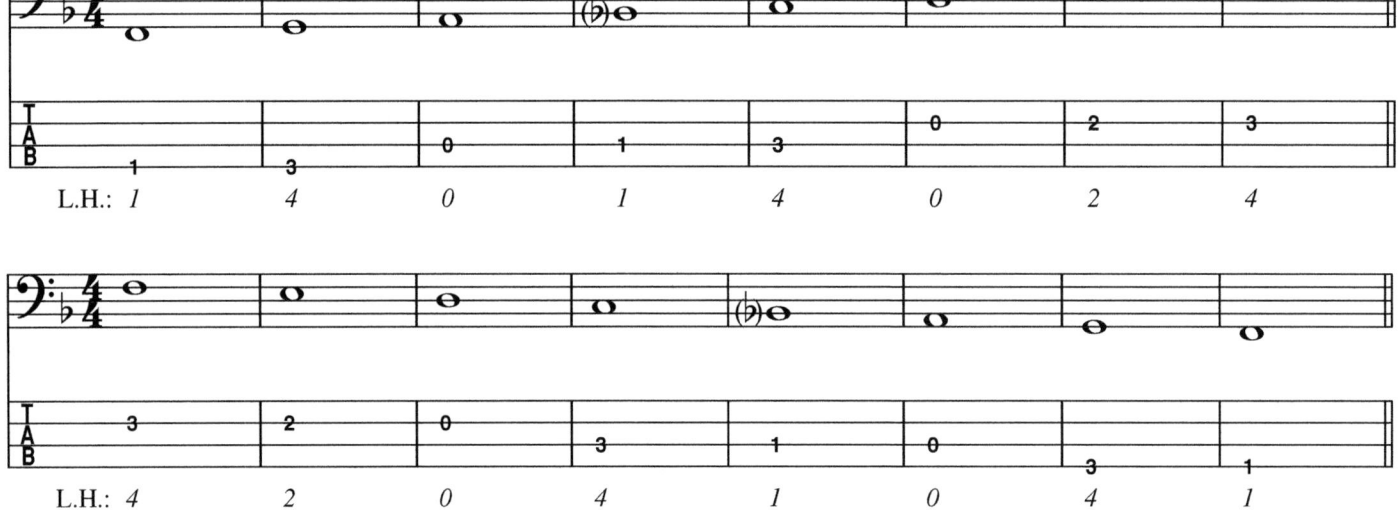

Exercise – F Major Scale

Remember that every B is flatted (♭) throughout the whole piece—even the one on the G string.

TRACK 33

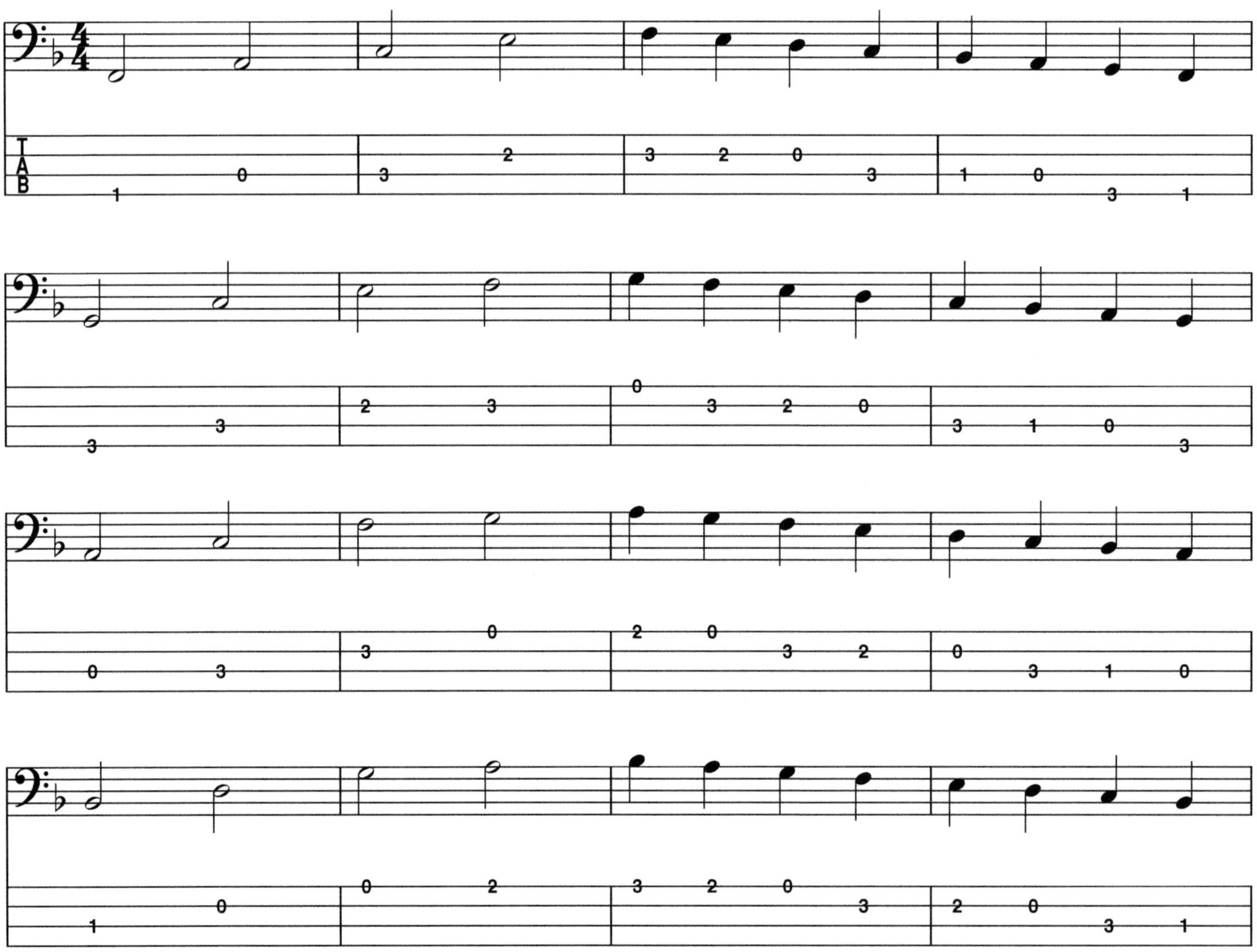

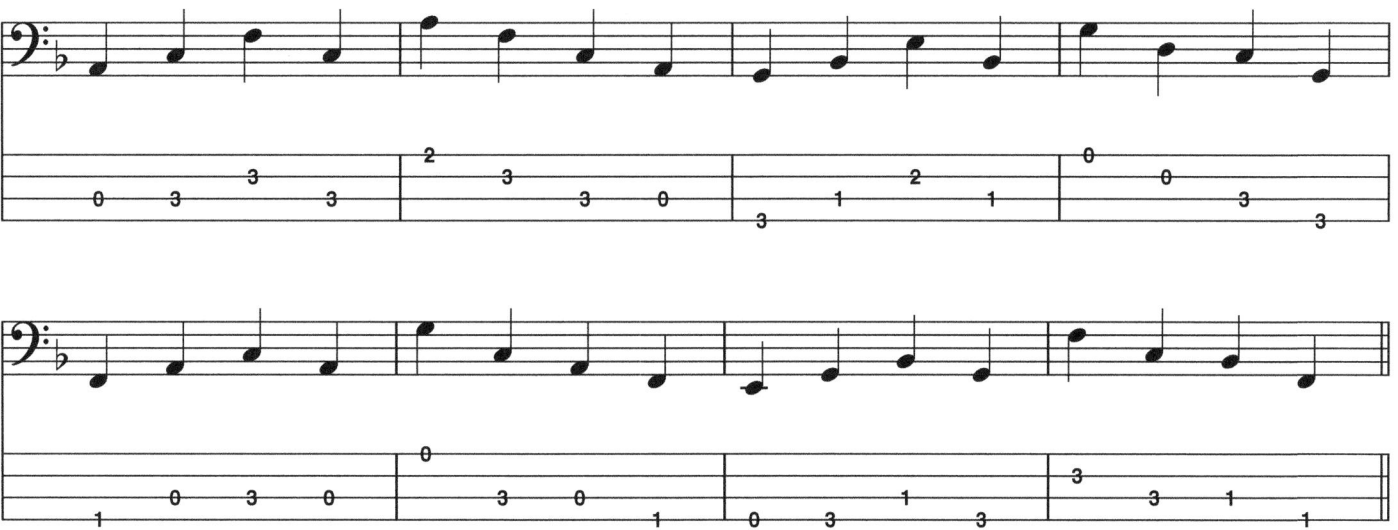

B♭ Major Scale

The key of B♭ contains two flats (B♭ and E♭). Again, practice the B♭ major scale (B♭–C–D–E♭–F–G–A–B♭) and try to play the scale as whole, half, quarter, and eighth notes.

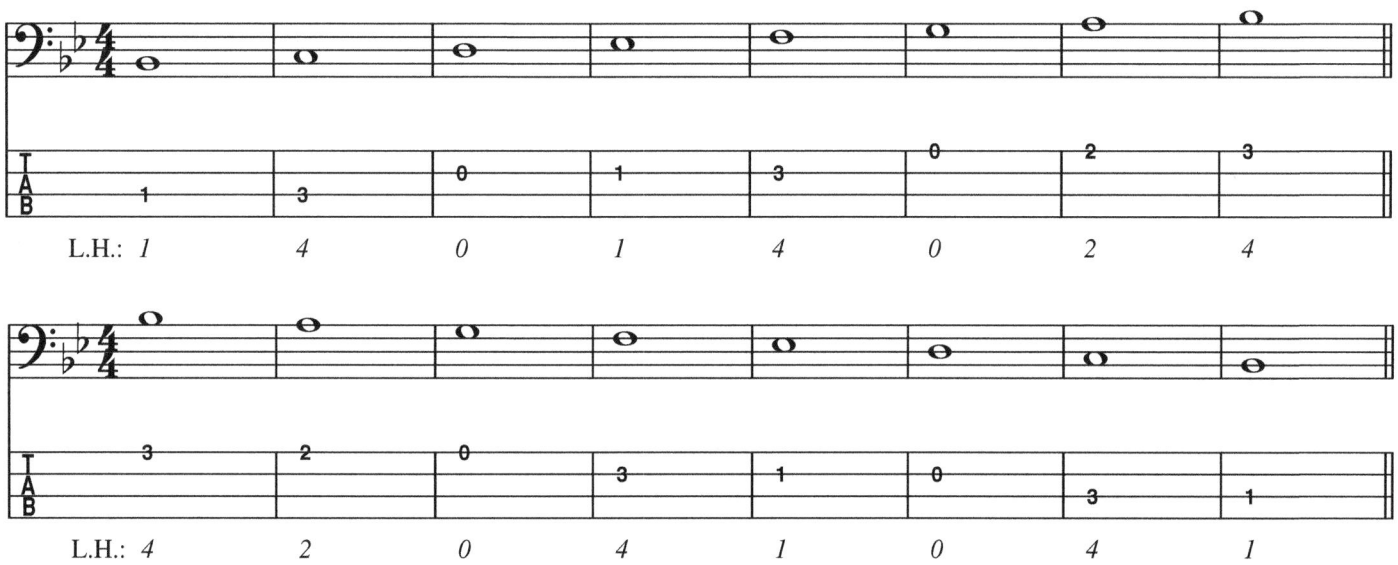

Exercise – B♭ Major Scale

TRACK 34

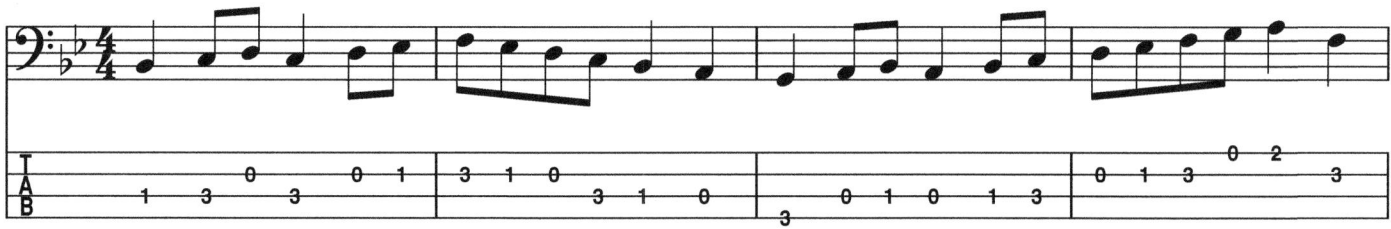

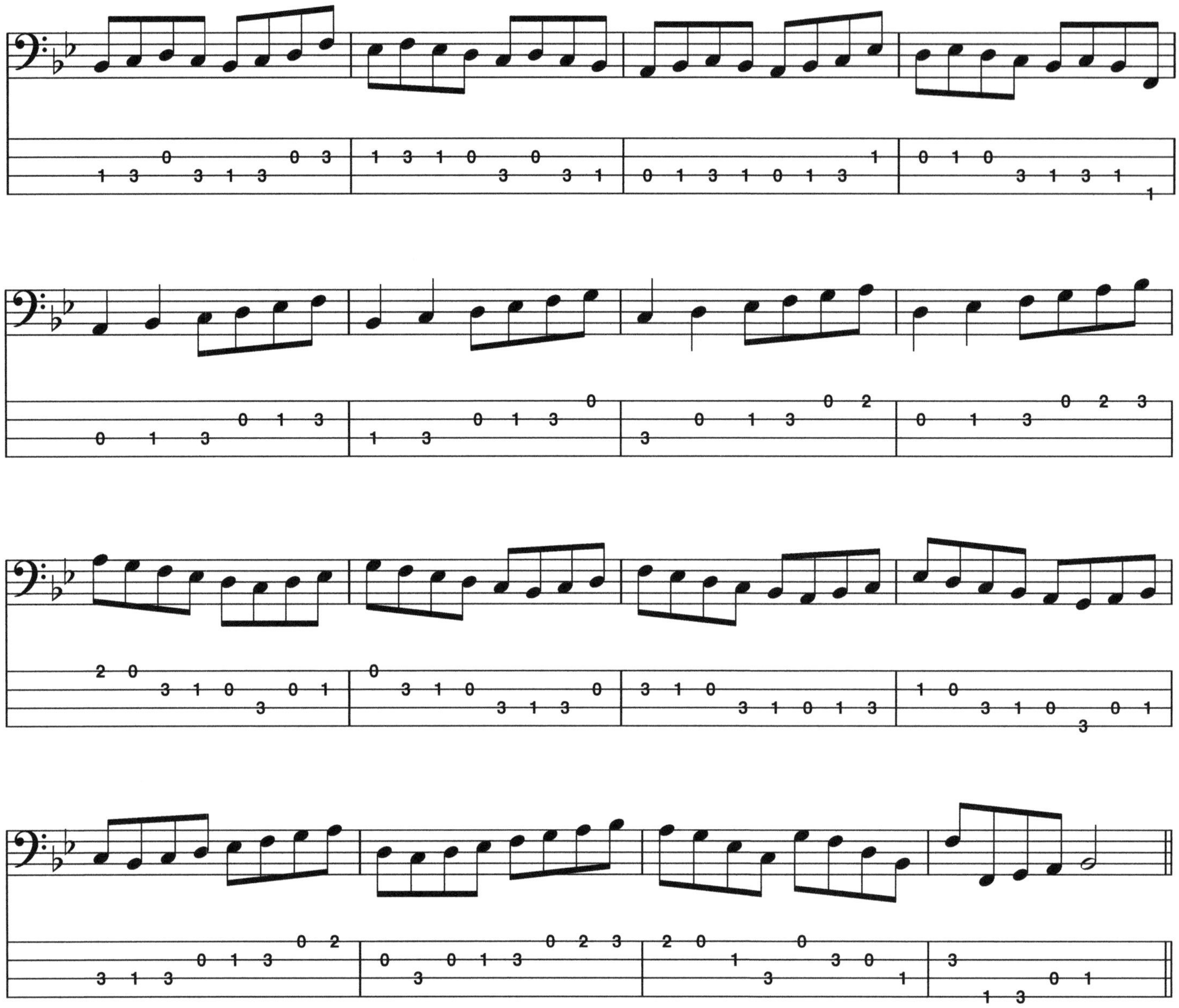

Boogie Woogie (12-Bar Blues)

The "boogie woogie" bass pattern is one of the most common bass patterns. It originated from the early days of stride piano in the 1920s. This blues is in the key of F. Every B is played as B♭. Be sure to watch the accidentals—they last only for the duration of the measure.

TRACK 35

46

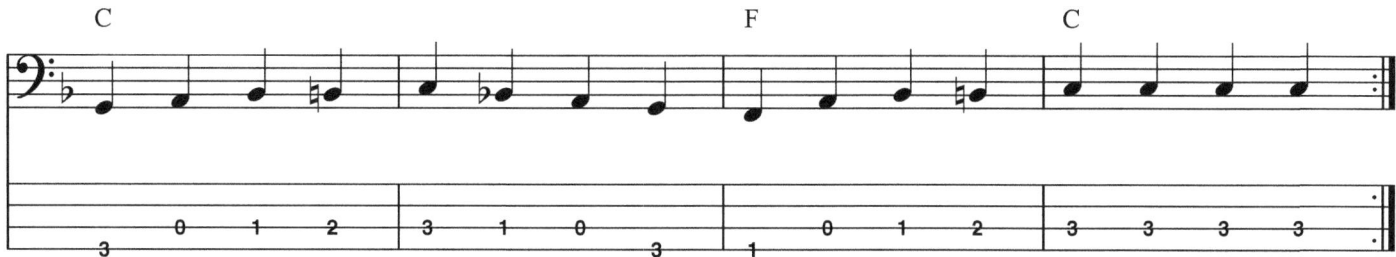

Walking Bass (12-Bar Blues)

The walking bass line is commonly heard in jazz. It's called a walking bass line because the rhythm is all quarter notes, and the line seems to be endlessly walking through the music. Watch those accidentals!

TRACK 36

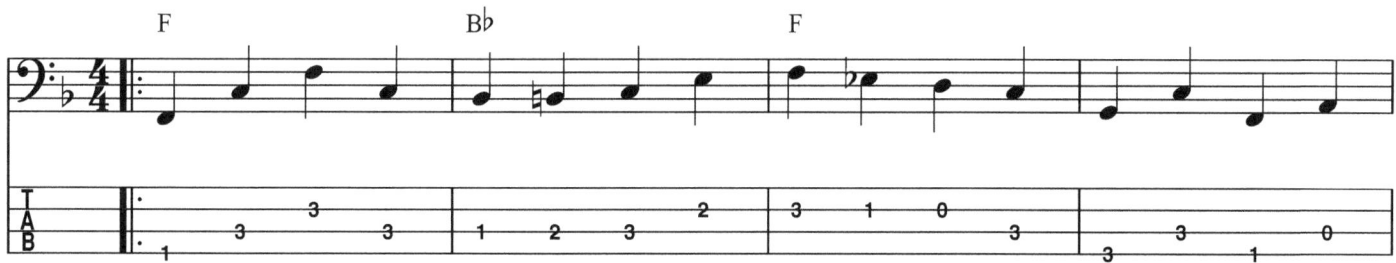

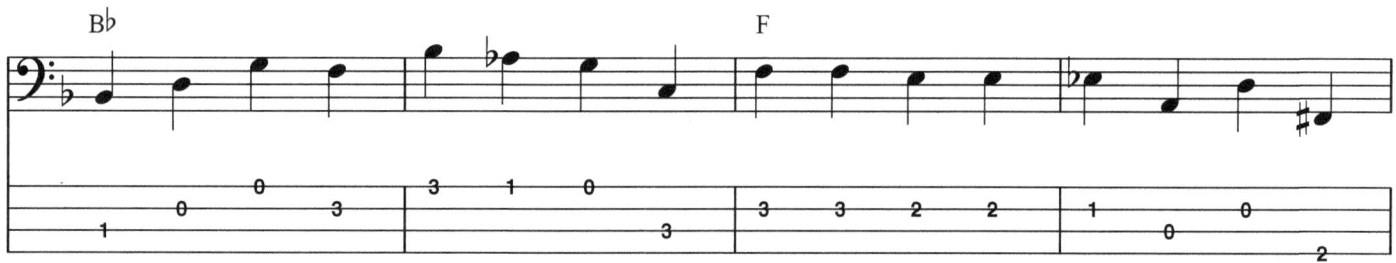

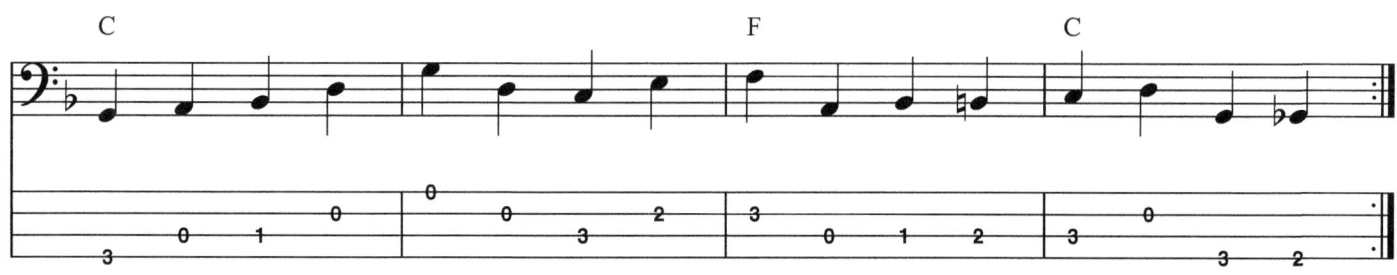

Movin' On Up: Playing the 2nd, 3rd, and 4th Frets

Move on up to the 2nd fret with your 1st finger. The following notes fall on the 2nd, 3rd, and 4th frets. While working through this position of the neck, be aware of the enharmonic equivalents.

Notes on the G String

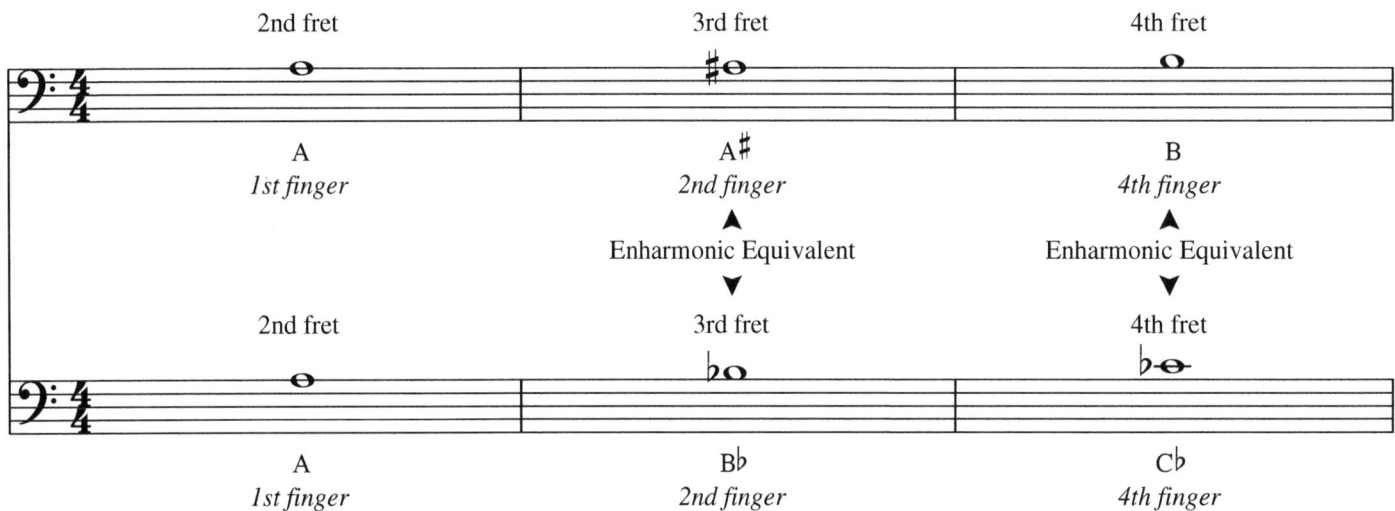

Exercise – G String

TRACK 37

Notes on the D String

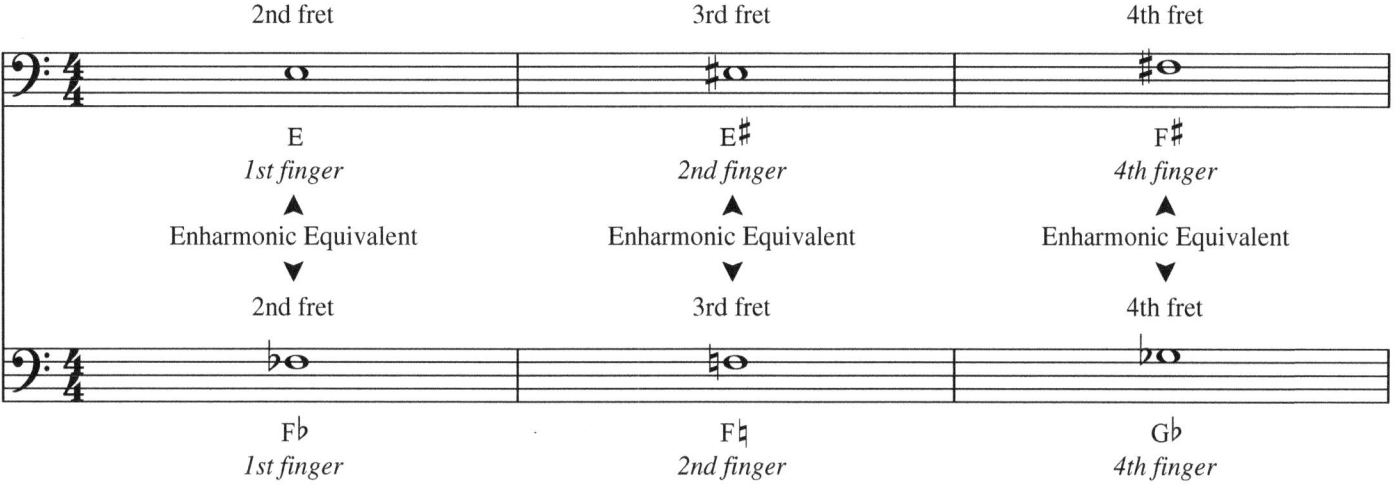

Exercise – D String

TRACK 38

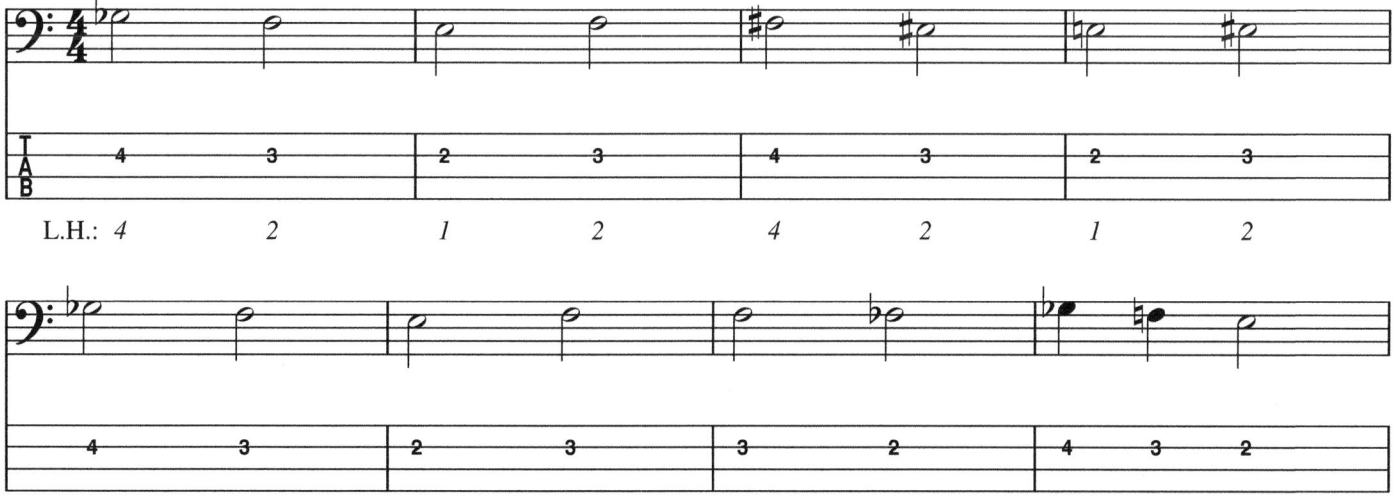

Notes on the A String

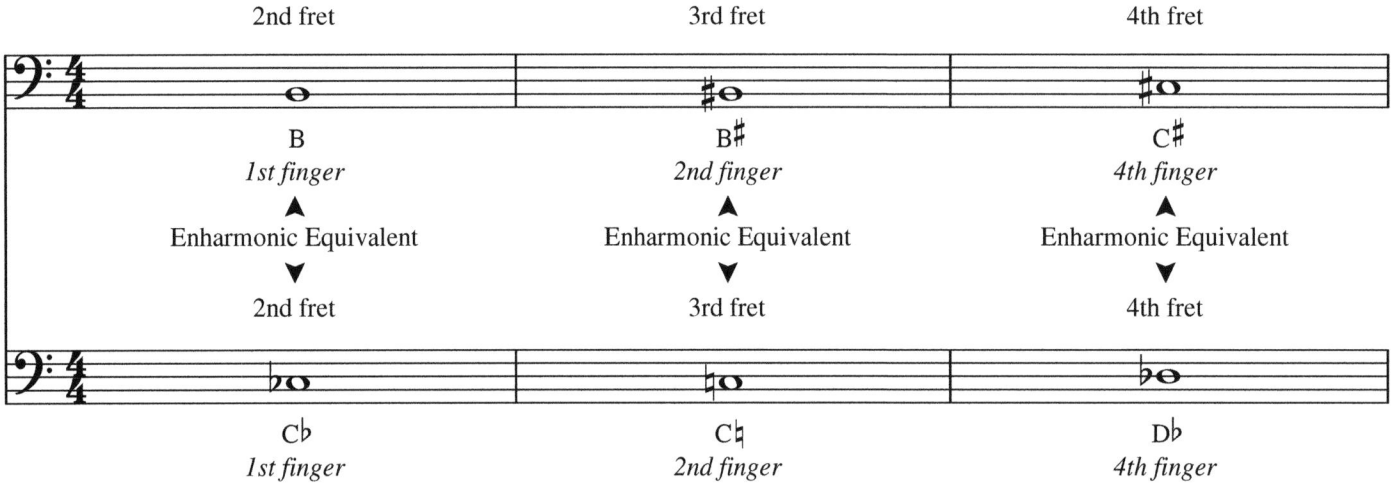

Exercise – A String

TRACK 39

Notes on the E String

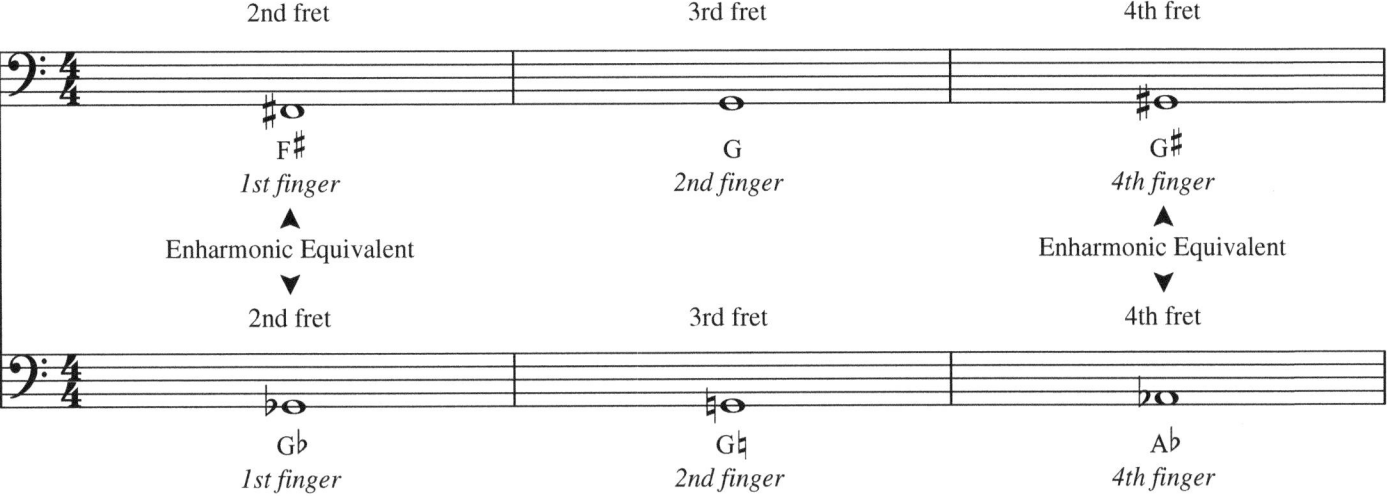

Exercise – E String

TRACK 40

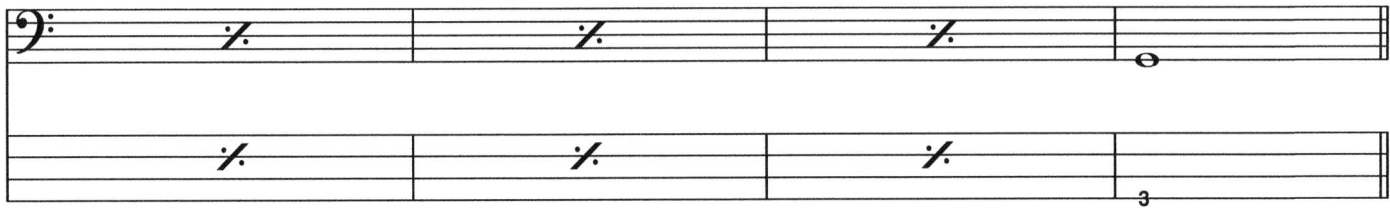

51

Using a Shift to Connect All Four Strings

Since we are using 1st, 2nd, and 4th fingers to play three consecutive notes, we will need to *shift* to play the notes beyond our three-fret reach. In the following example, concentrate on keeping your fingers together as a unit while you shift to reach the next note.

In measure 2, you'll shift to the 1st fret with your 1st finger. Then, on beat 3 of measure 3, you'll shift back up to the 4th fret with your 4th finger. The rest of the exercise continues in a similar manner. The best way to get a feel for the shift is to *shift from your thumb*—your fingers will naturally follow. Take it slow, gradually increasing the speed.

TRACK 41

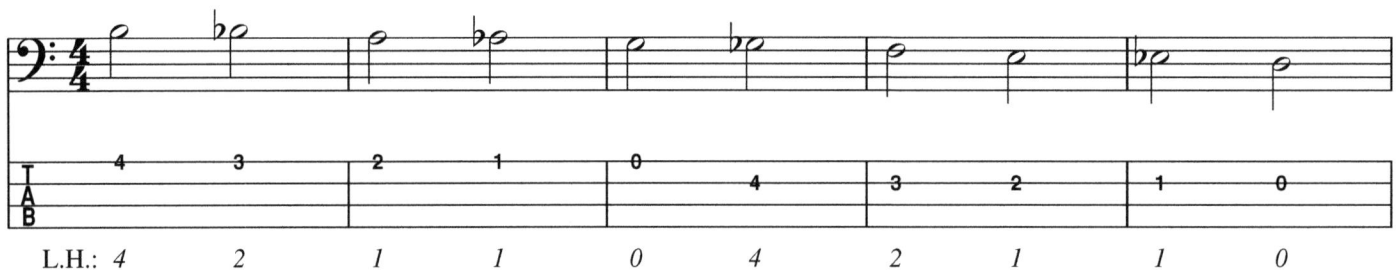

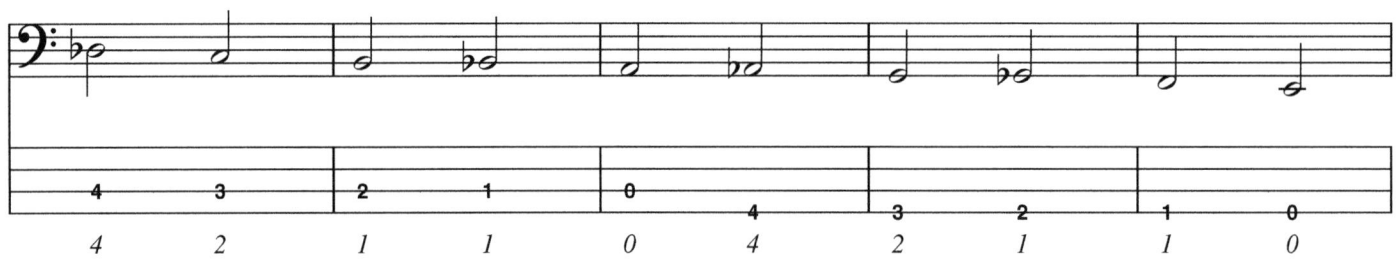

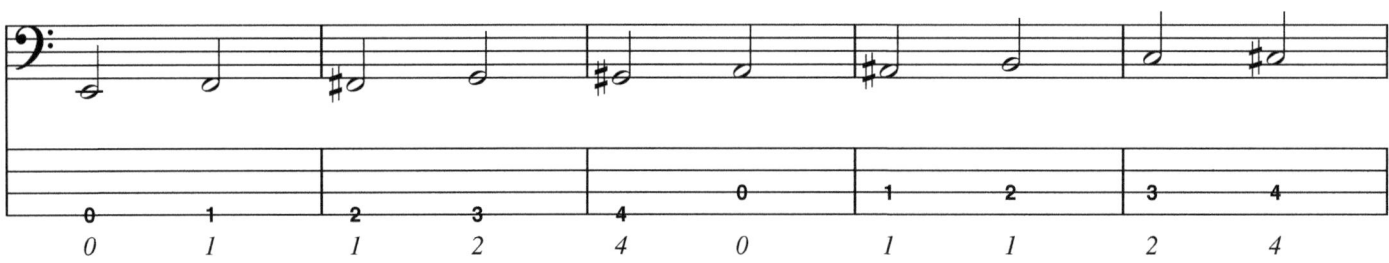

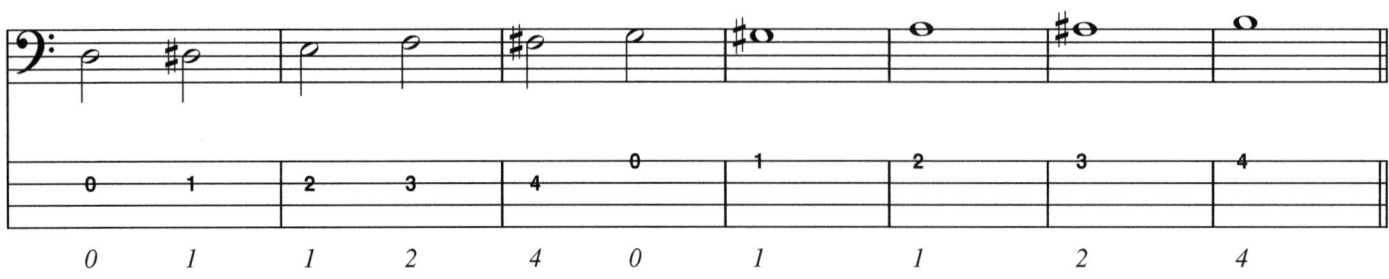

G Major Scale

The key of G major contains one sharp (F♯). Practice the G major scale (G–A–B–C–D–E–F♯–G) from the 2nd-fret position. Try saying aloud the names of the notes as you play them.

Exercise – G Major Scale

Play the following exercise in 2nd position. Be sure to count—the last four bars are syncopated and notice that there's always a rest on beat 2. (See page 107 for more on syncopation.)

TRACK 42

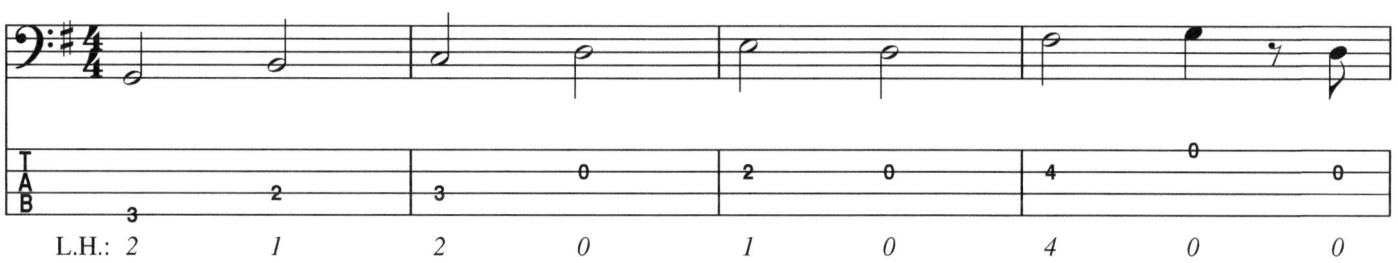

The following exercise is in the key of C. In measure 1, start in 1st position, at the 1st fret, and shift up to the 2nd fret for the 2nd measure.

TRACK 43

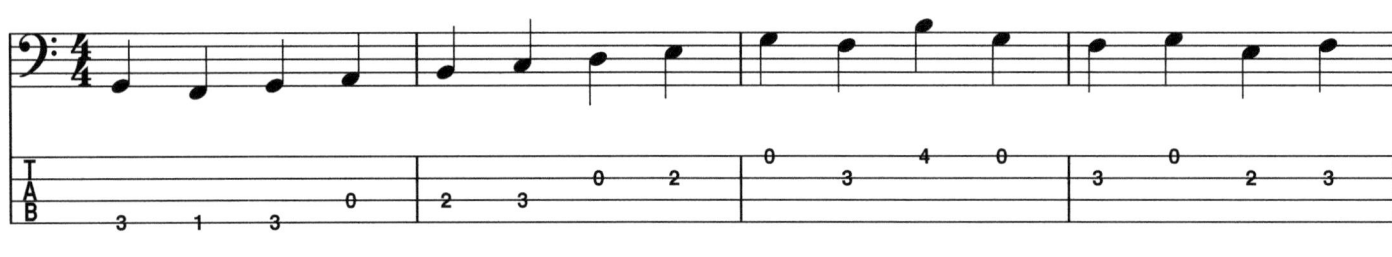

A Major Scale

The key of A major contains three sharps (F♯, C♯, and G♯). Start the A major scale (A–B–C♯–D–E–F♯–G♯–A) from the 2nd-fret position, shifting back to the 1st fret for the final G♯–A. Practice saying aloud the names of the notes as you play them.

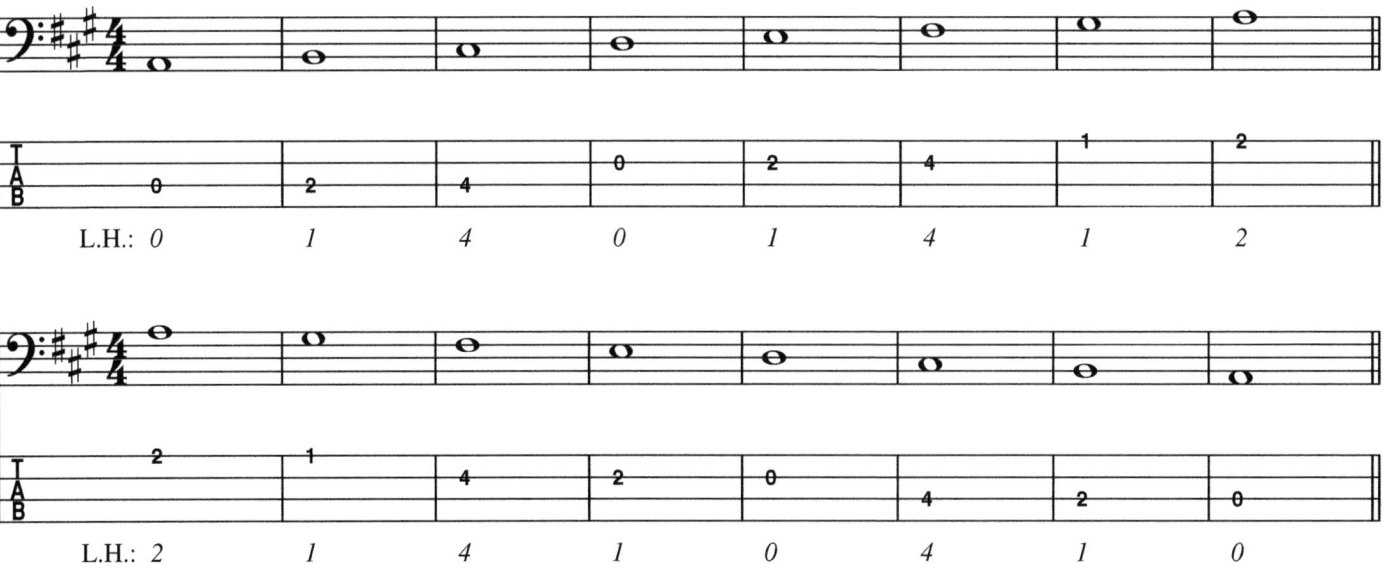

Exercise – A Major Scale

Start this exercise in the 2nd-fret position. Be mindful of the accidentals throughout, as well as the poppin' in the final three measures.

54

TRACK 44

12-Bar Blues

Play the majority of this exercise in the 2nd-fret position. You'll need to shift to the 1st fret for the A♯, F, and D♯ in measures 2, 10, and 11, respectively. Make sure that you count through the rhythms of this blues; the triplets are played three notes to a beat, and the dotted eighth–16th note patterns create the shuffle feel. If you need to refresh your memory, jump back to the Playing the Open Strings section and replay the Triplet and Shuffle Rhythm exercises. Don't forget about the repeat sign at the end of the song.

TRACK 45

Triplet Exercise

If you were unable to complete the last exercise, STOP! Go back and work on the bass line until you have mastered the rhythms. The next exercise contains only triplets and shuffle rhythms. They sound very similar, but they are different.

Start by playing this exercise in 1st position, using your 2nd and 4th fingers. Once you feel comfortable, challenge yourself by switching to the 2nd-fret position. Now play the bass line with your 1st and 2nd fingers. (You'll need to shift to the 1st fret to play the B♭ in measure 9.)

TRACK 46

Basic Blues Pattern in G

Here's another blues pattern. Play this at the 2nd fret and don't forget to repeat the pattern.

TRACK 47

Using Pentatonic Scales

The *pentatonic scale* is one of the most popular scales used in music. Consisting of only five notes, we create it by removing the 4th and 7th notes of any major scale. The remaining five notes make up the *major pentatonic scale*. The following is a C major pentatonic scale (C–D–E–G–A–C).

C Major Scale

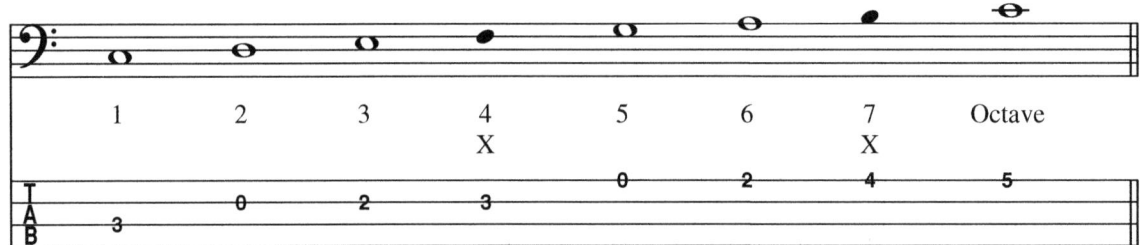

C Major Pentatonic Scale

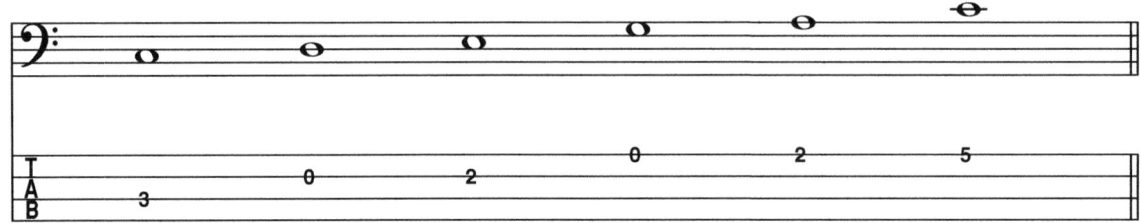

Playing a groove in C major pentatonic is easy—just stay in 2nd position. The only shift you'll need to make is for the high C on the G string in measure 2. Shift back to 2nd position for measures 3 and 4.

TRACK 48

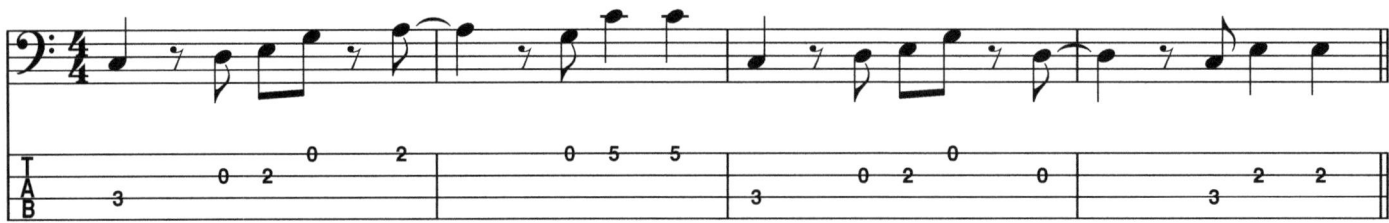

You can start on any note of the scale to create different scales. If you start the same group of notes on the fifth note (A), it creates an *A minor pentatonic scale* (A–C–D–E–G–A).

A Minor Pentatonic Scale

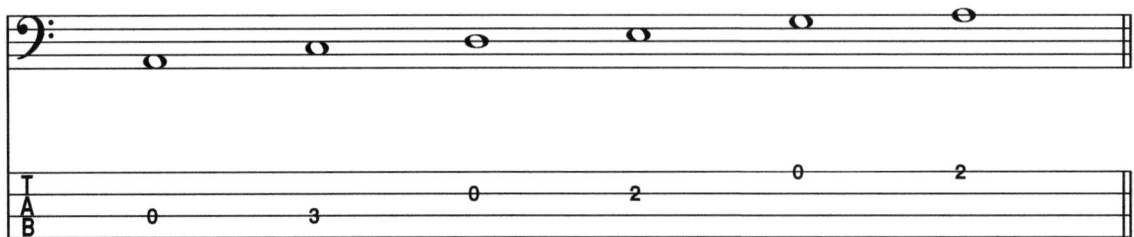

58

A minor pentatonic can be played in the same position as C major. This lick uses some of the poppin' technique that you learned earlier. Practice it with your fingers first. When you have the feel of it, add the poppin' with your right hand. In the 2nd measure, there is a short slide to E on the D string; play this note with your 1st finger.

TRACK 49

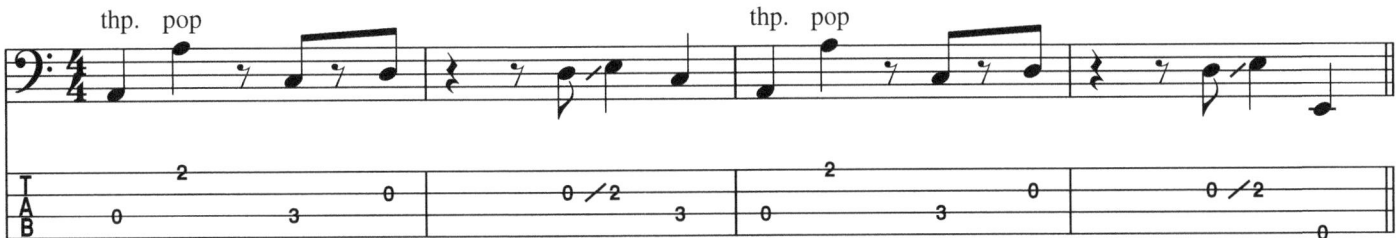

The following examples use pentatonic scales over the frets that we have studied. Practice them and become accustomed to their sound. After you are acquainted with the fingering and the sound, create your own bass patterns, using only the notes from each scale.

Example 1

This mode comes from the A♭ major pentatonic scale (A♭–B♭–C–E♭–F–A♭). By starting on F, it creates an F minor pentatonic scale (F–A♭–B♭–C–E♭–F). The notes on the G string were added so that you can play across all four strings. You'll have to shift up to the 4th fret for the A♭.

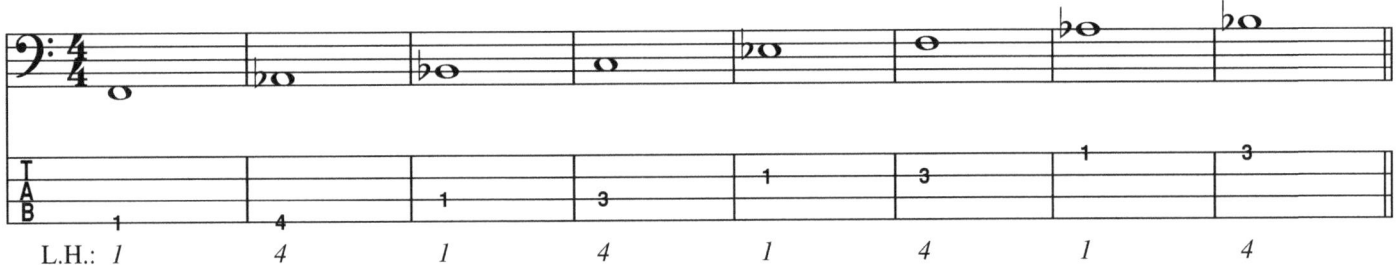

This is a great exercise to develop your shifting and pinky strength.

TRACK 50

Now try moving that groove up to the next group of strings (A–D and D–G). It can also be played up the neck— try it at the 3rd, 5th, and 7th frets!

Example 2

This next mode is based on the B♭ major pentatonic (B♭–C–D–F–G–B♭) scale. Starting on the fifth note (G) makes this a G minor pentatonic scale (G–B♭–C–D–F–G).

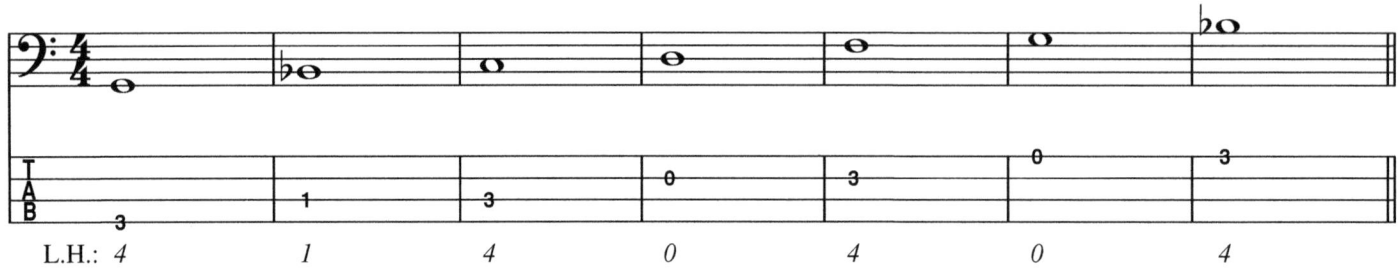

The following is a great groove. You can use it over G7 or G minor chords. Be careful of the rhythm here. No notes are attacked on beats 3 and 4; they're held over from the previous beats. It's the rhythm that makes the groove!

TRACK 51

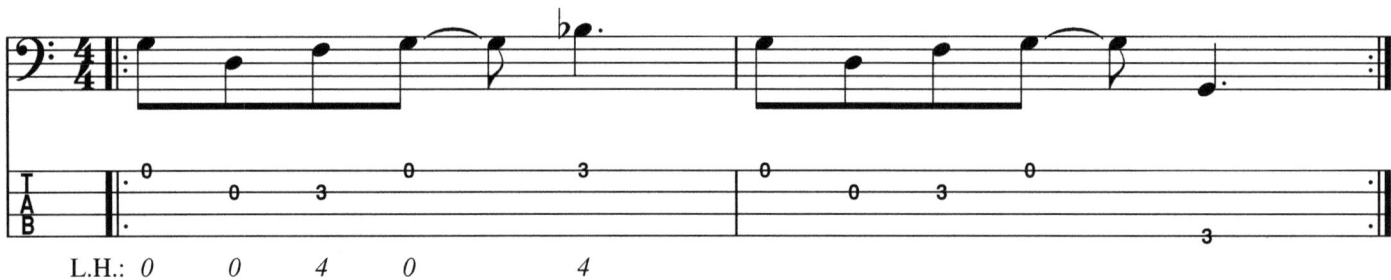

Example 3

This example uses B♭ minor pentatonic (B♭–D♭–E♭–F–A♭–B♭). You'll need to shift up for the D♭ at the 4th fret. Can you figure out which major pentatonic it comes from? (Hint: Look for the relationship of the major and minor scales from the earlier examples.)

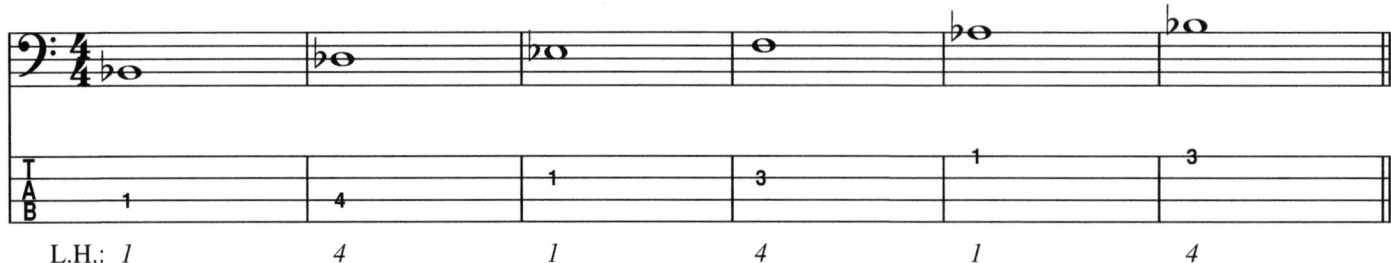

Here you'll be shifting back and forth between the 1st and 4th frets. Measures 3–4 repeat the first two bars.

Example 4

This example uses the C minor pentatonic scale (C–E♭–F–G–B♭–C) across all of the strings. For the last two notes (B♭–C), shift up to the 3rd fret with your 1st finger for the B♭, then play the C with your 4th finger.

Can you figure out which major pentatonic this minor scale is from?

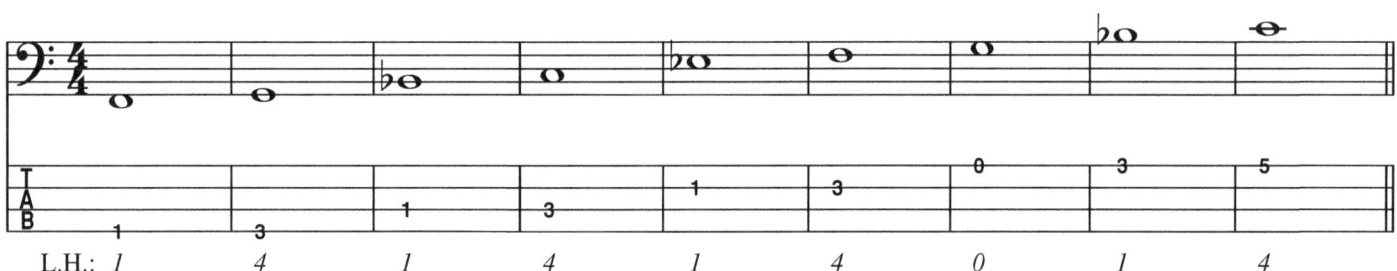

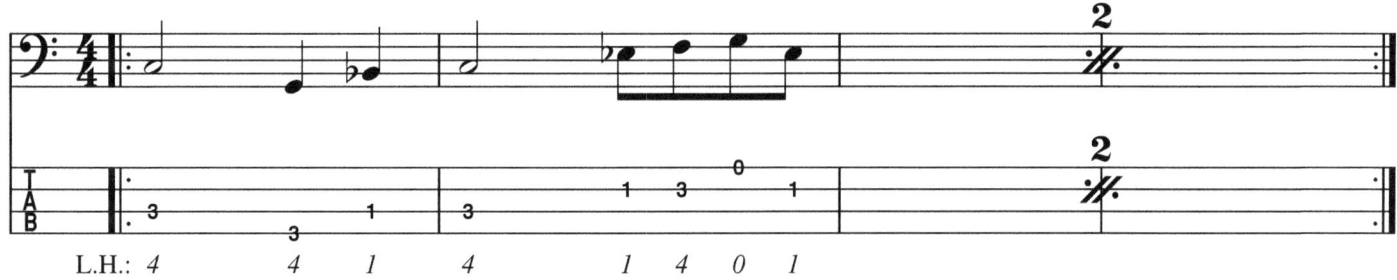

Get creative with these lines. Once you get the hang of this C minor lick, try playing the 1st measure up an octave, with the C, G, and B♭ notes all on the G string, then drop down to the C on the A string in measure 2.

Well, did you figure out the major pentatonic scales in Examples 3 and 4? The B♭ minor pentatonic comes from the D♭ major pentatonic scale, and C minor pentatonic comes from the E♭ major pentatonic scale.

Summary Exercises on the 1st, 2nd, 3rd, and 4th Frets

The following exercises summarize the fingerings and shifts covered so far. Make sure that you're comfortable not only playing the notes, but reading them, as well.

TRACK 54

TRACK 55

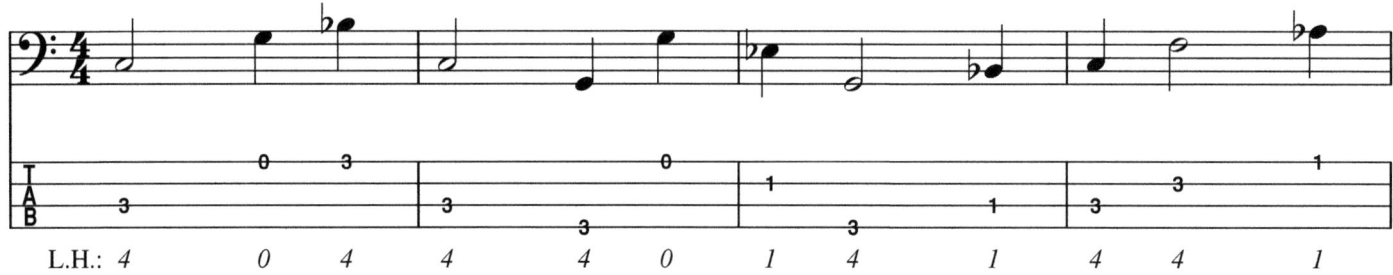

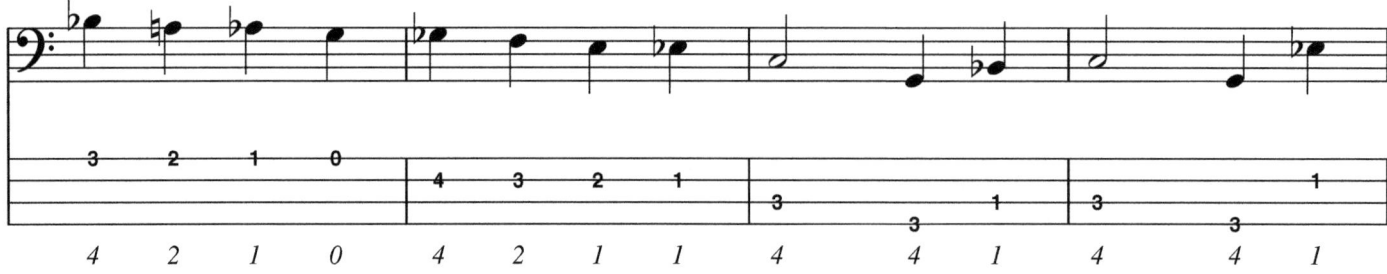

This example opens up the possibilities of playing across all of the strings in your bass lines.

TRACK 56

Grooves

Here are two good grooves that utilize the positions that we've studied thus far.

Groove A

This bass line utilizes open strings and keeps a steady pulse. The opening rhythm may look tricky, but it's easy if you look for beats 1 and 3. We'll use the shuffle variation that was discussed earlier (see page 25) to get the right feel. Be sure to count to keep your place! In measure 29, play the B♮–C–C♯ with your 1st, 2nd, and 4th fingers, respectively.

TRACK 57

Slowly and Strong

Groove B

The rhythm of the intro is identical to Groove A, and the majority of the song will be played at the 1st fret. In measures 5–11, be careful of the rhythms. All of the notes in the measures are on the downbeat, except on beat 4—the note is attacked just after the downbeat, on the second 16th note. In measure 14, shift up to the B♭ with your 1st finger; this puts you in position for the rest of the measure. In measure 15, shift back down for the A♭. In measure 24, play both the C and the B♭ with your 4th finger. Remember to keep all of your fingers on the G string for stability.

TRACK 58

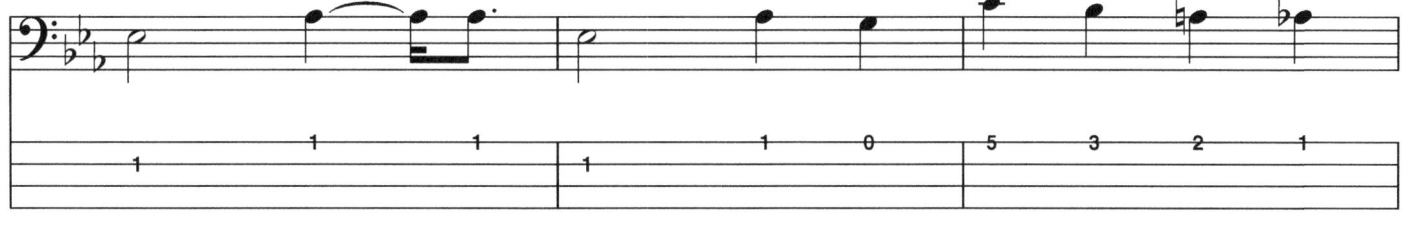

Repeat and fade

Movin' On Up: Playing the 3rd, 4th, and 5th Frets

Notes on the G String

Take your time with the enharmonics on this string. Remember: there are two names for each note—it can get confusing!

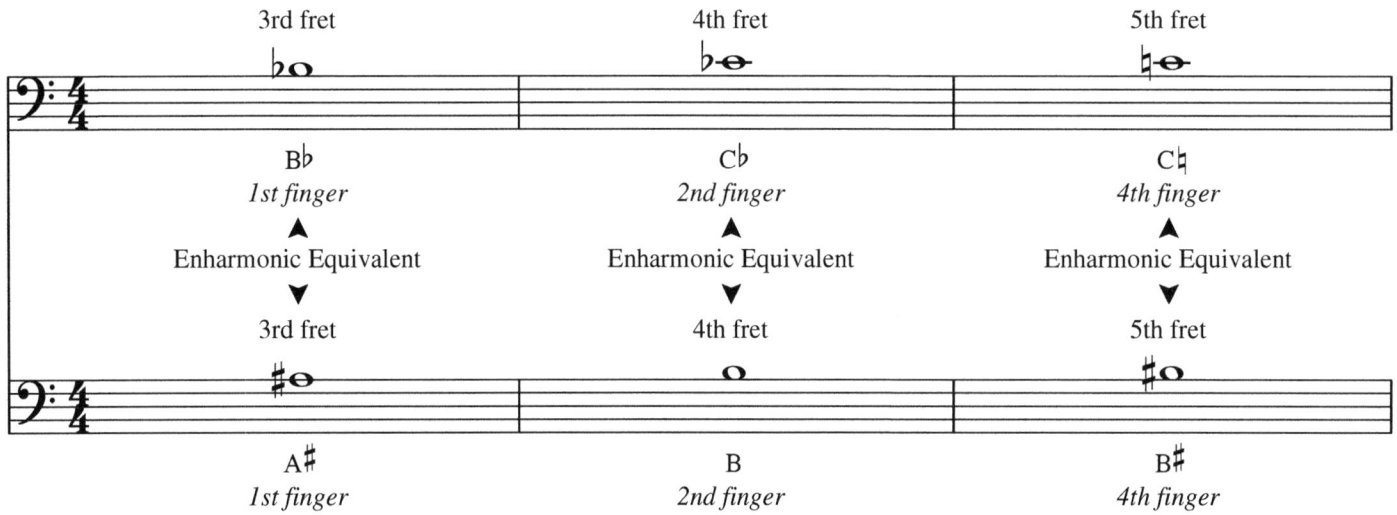

Exercise – G String

TRACK 59

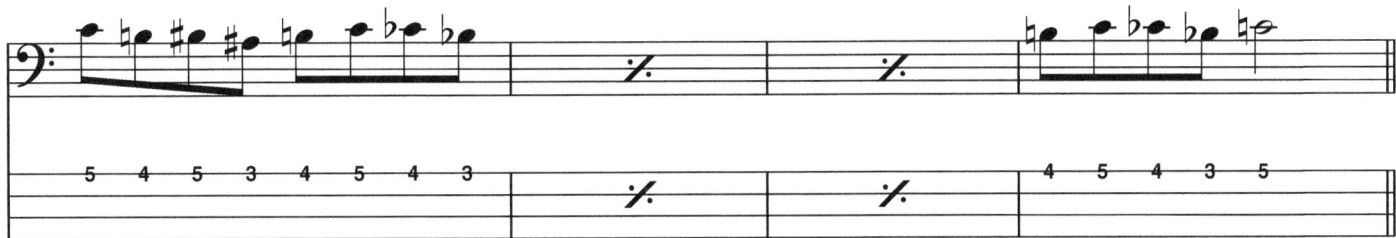

Notes on the D String

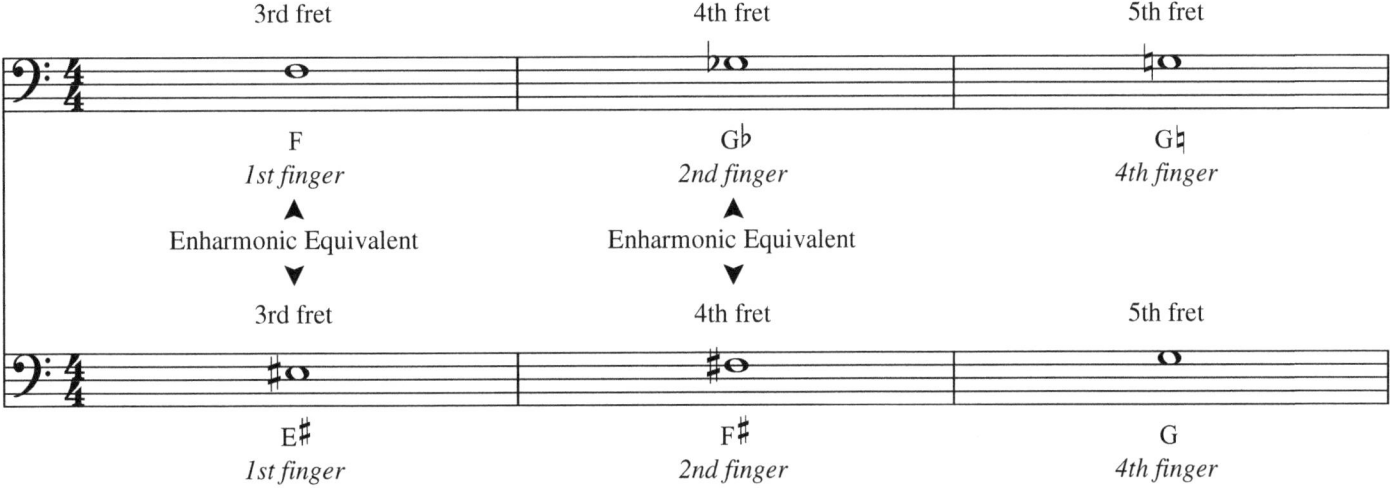

Exercise – D String

TRACK 60

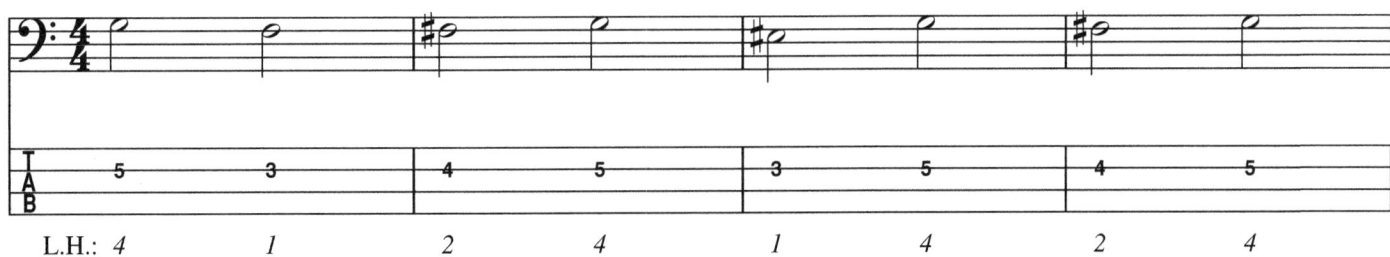

L.H.: 4   1   2   4   1   4   2   4

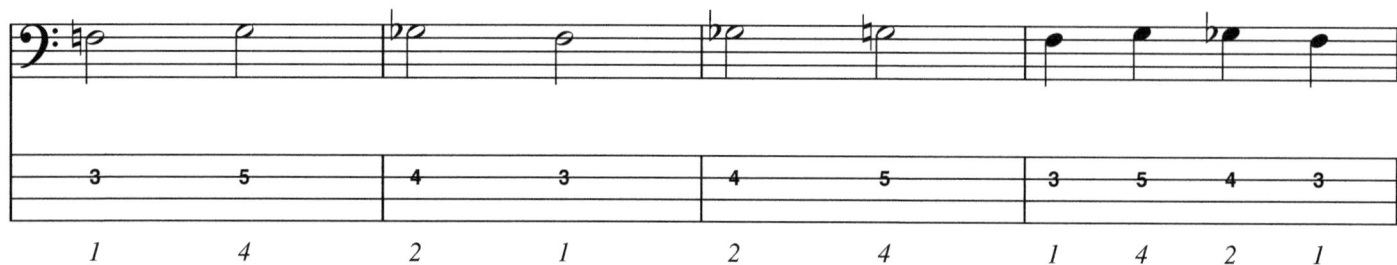

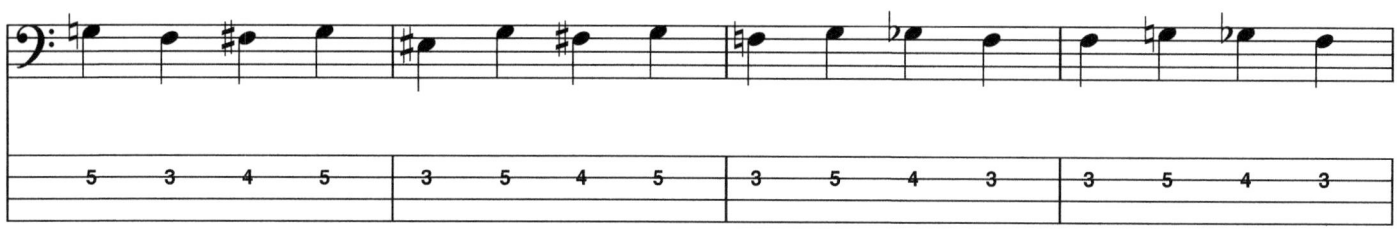

Notes on the A String

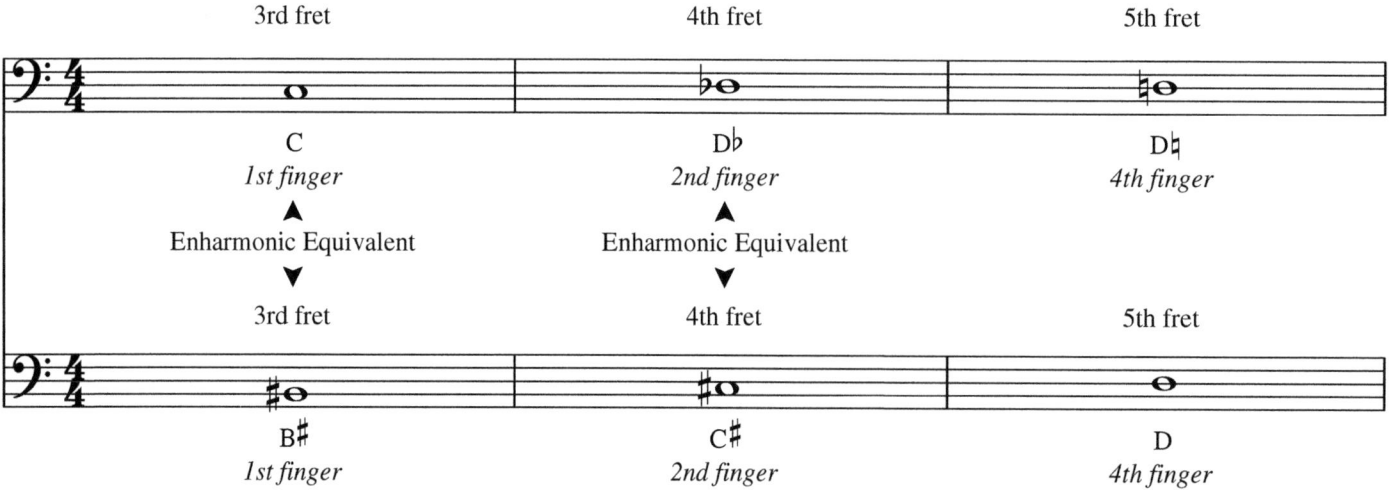

Exercise – A String

TRACK 61

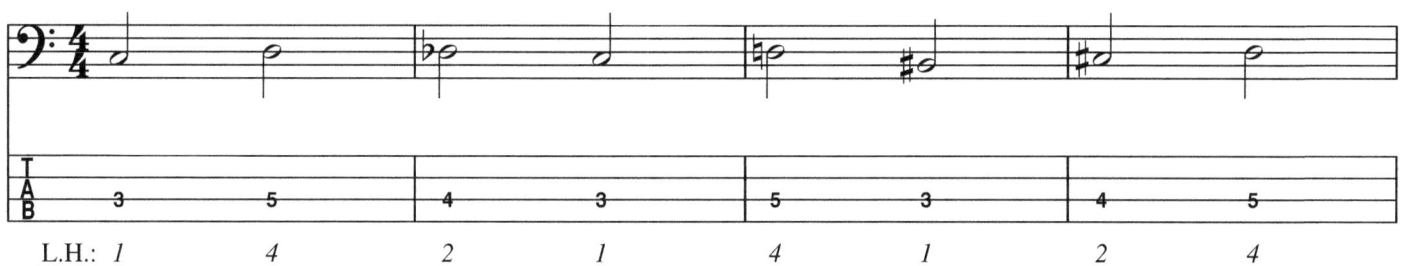

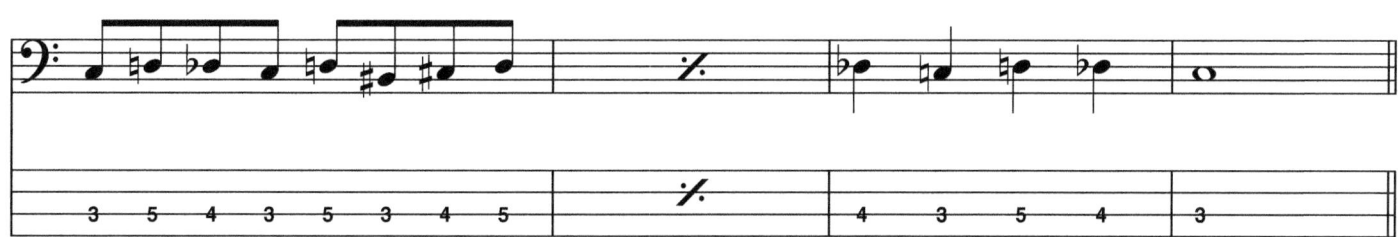

Notes on the E String

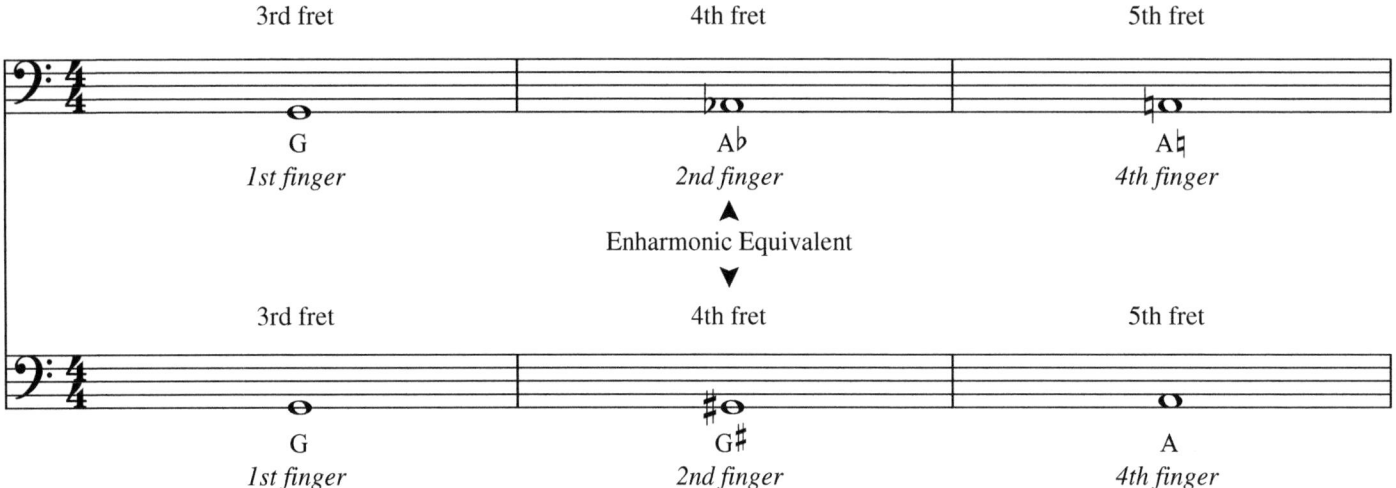

Exercise – E String

TRACK 62

Connecting All Four Strings

TRACK 63

There is a pop and thump at the end of this example. Play the G-string hammer-on and quickly move your 1st finger to the A string.

TRACK 64

C Major Scale

There are no flats or sharps in the key of C major, but there will be shifts in the scale to reach the C on the G string. Make sure you're comfortable with the shifting in the scale before moving on.

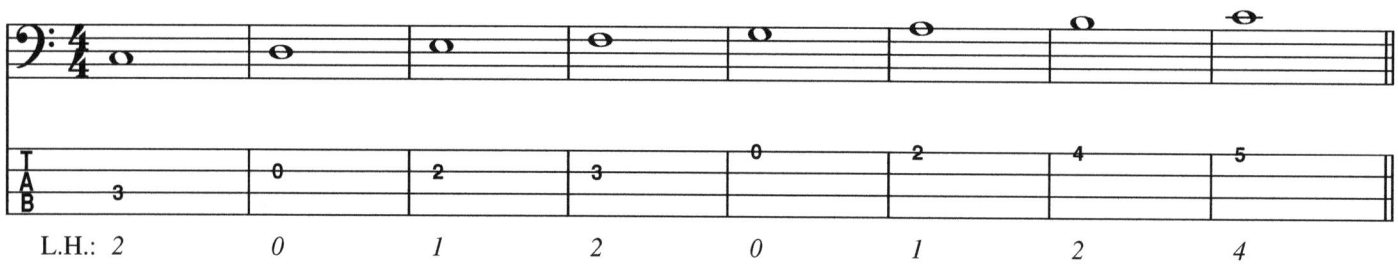

L.H.: 2   0   1   2   0   1   2   4

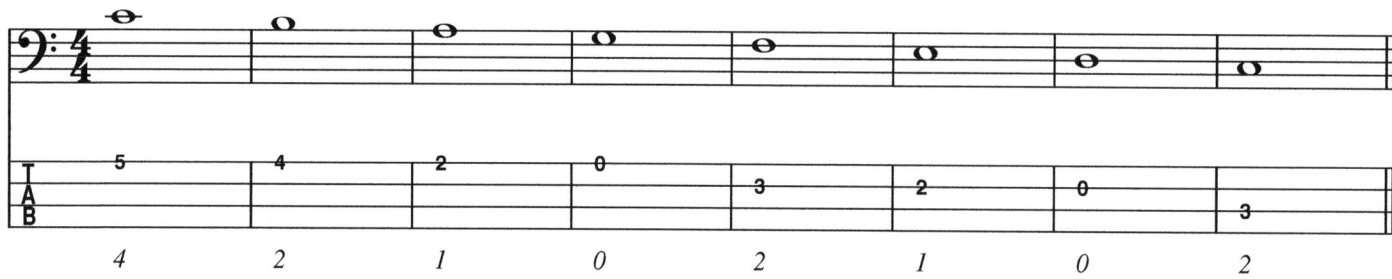

4   2   1   0   2   1   0   2

Exercise – C Major Scale

Start this exercise slowly. Once you're comfortable, challenge yourself to see how fast you can play it. It starts slowly but it gets more complex at the end!

TRACK 65

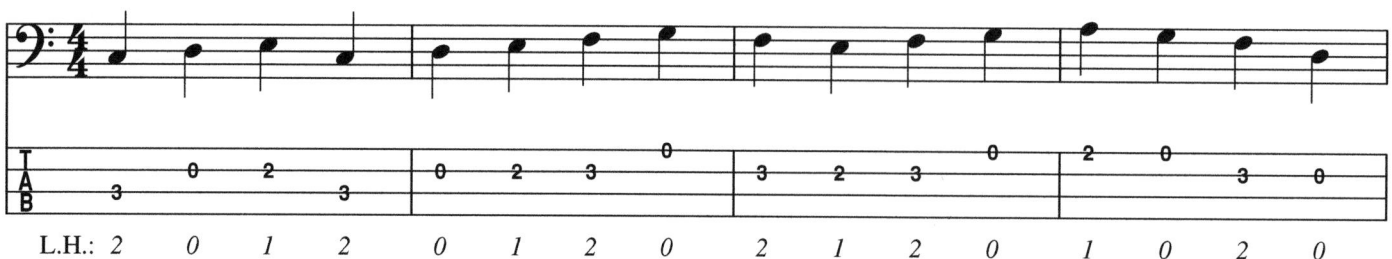

L.H.: 2   0   1   2   0   1   2   0   2   1   2   0   1   0   2   0

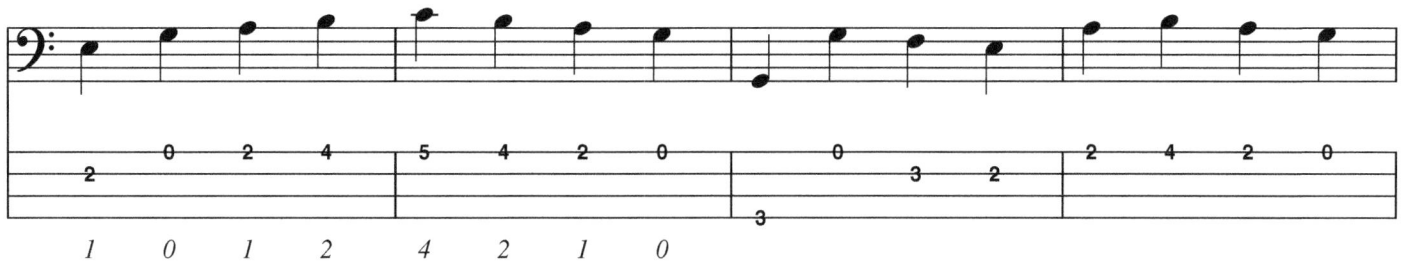
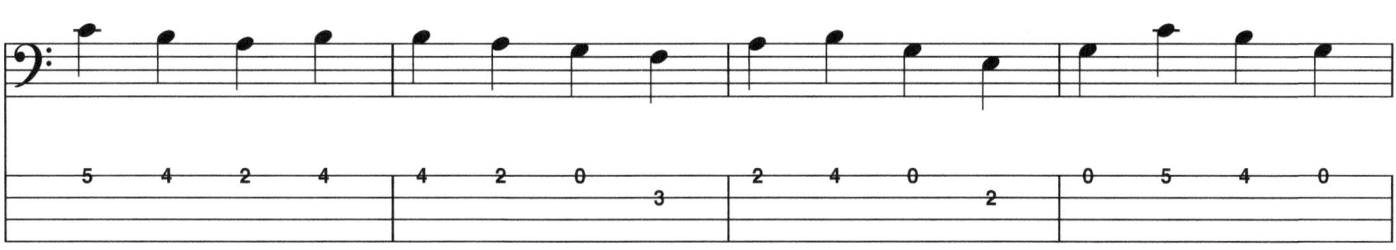

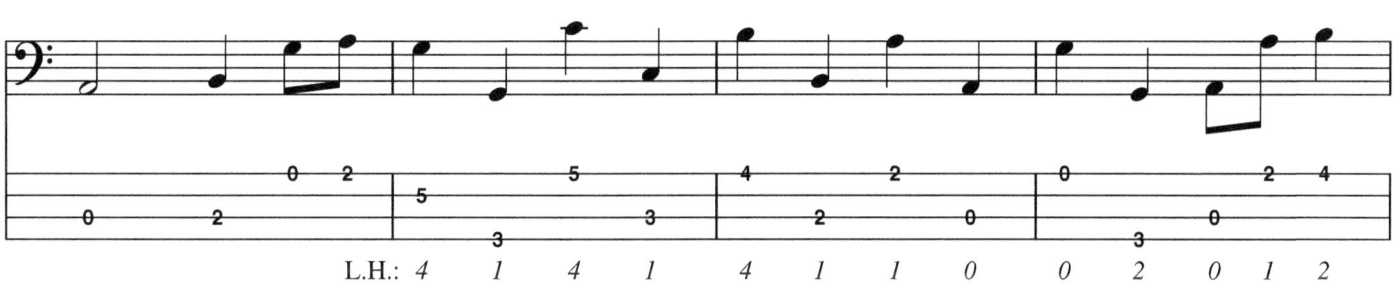
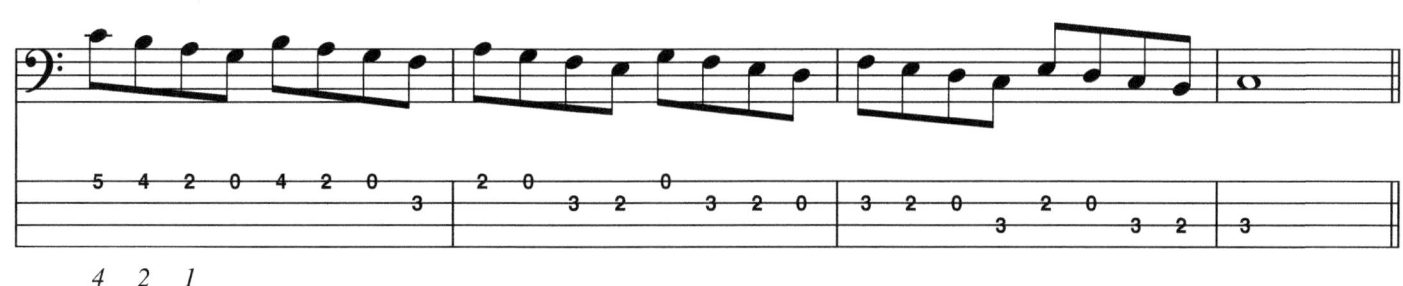

Thumpin' & Poppin' in Octaves

This section uses the same techniques that we looked at earlier in the book and plays through the 1st-, 2nd-, and 3rd-fret positions. In all of these bass grooves, the idea is to keep your 1st finger on the lower strings while using your 4th finger to play the notes on the higher strings. It will help to keep your 1st finger straight and curl your 3rd and 4th fingers to reach the top strings. Remember to shift with your thumb—your fingers will always follow!

Poppin' the right hand will be the same as before; use your thumb to *thump* the lower notes and your index/middle fingers to *pop* the upper notes. If you haven't gotten comfortable with the poppin' technique yet, you can still play all of these grooves by simply alternating your index and middle fingers, as in the earlier exercises.

Work each groove slowly, taking it one pass at a time. As you build your strength, try repeating each line multiple times. For a marathon workout, try moving from one repeated groove to the next without stopping!

E-String and D-String Grooves

Let's get going! This groove moves up the E and D strings. Keep your 1st finger straight and shift up with your thumb. In the last measure, pop the hammer-on on beat 3 and thump the last note.

TRACK 66

TRACK 67

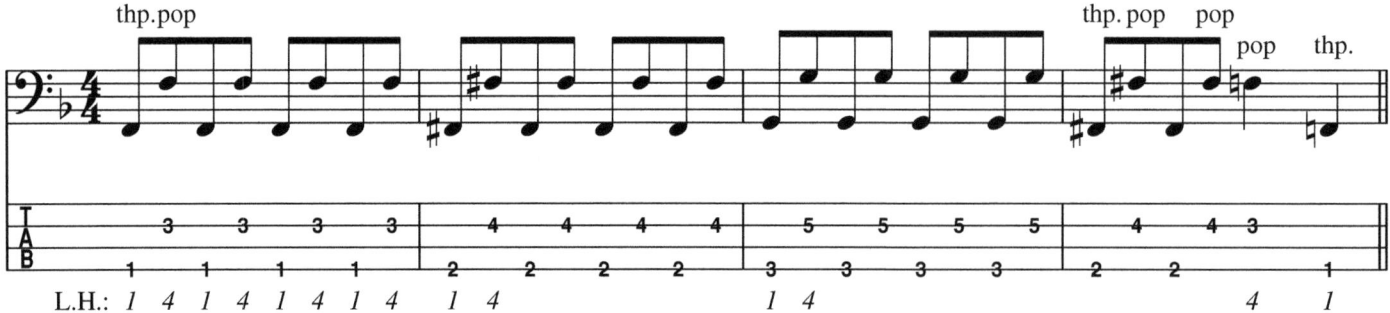

TRACK 68

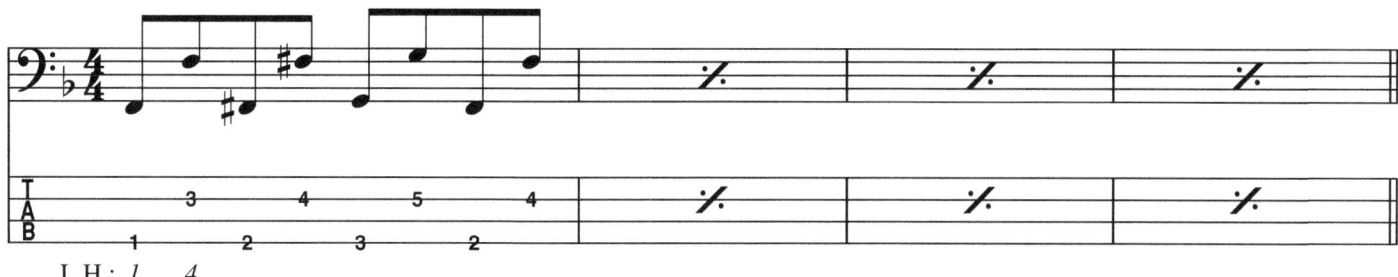

As in the first groove, beat 3 starts with a pop on the D string and ends with a thump on the E string. Be sure to count, as the "and" of beat 3 is held over for all of beat 4.

TRACK 69

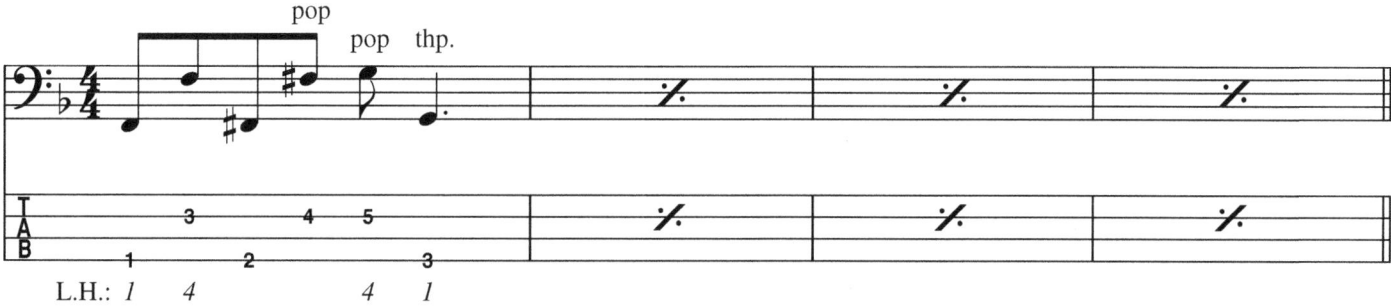

Take your time with the poppin' in this groove. This example will require a thump and a pop *on the same string*. Simply thump the E♭ on the D string, then pop the F on the same string, and follow up with a thump on the E string. This poppin' pattern will continue throughout the groove.

TRACK 70

The same poppin' approach applies here.

TRACK 71

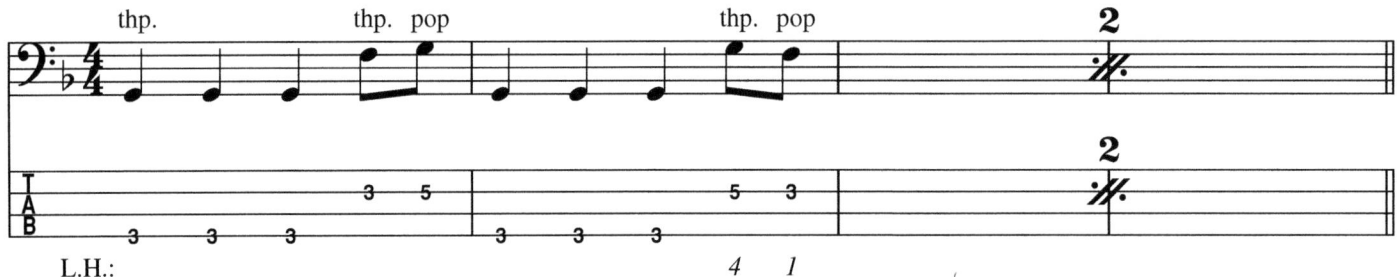

The poppin' groove reverses in measure 5. In the last measure, use the same-string thump/pop method.

TRACK 72

Grooves on the A and G Strings

TRACK 73

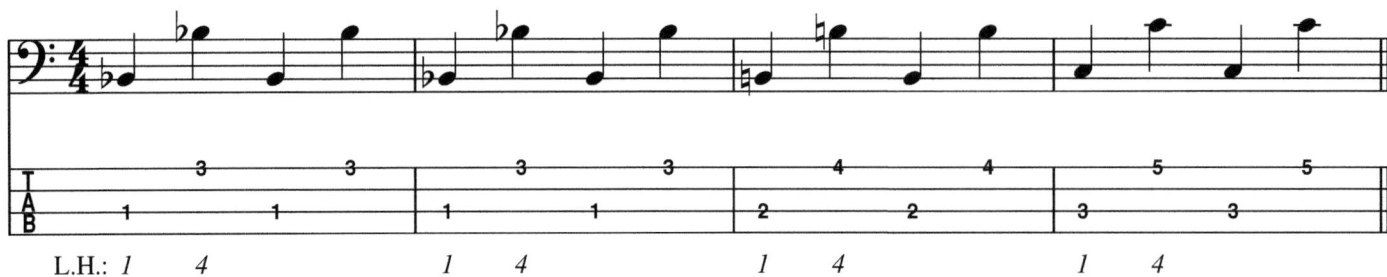

This groove includes notes on the E and D strings.

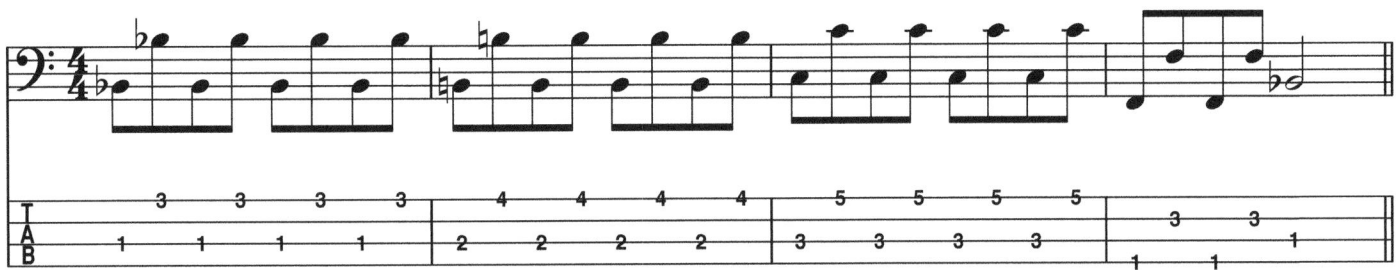

In measures 1–4, beat 4 will change poppin' patterns. Just remember that the lower strings get the thumb, and the upper strings get popped.

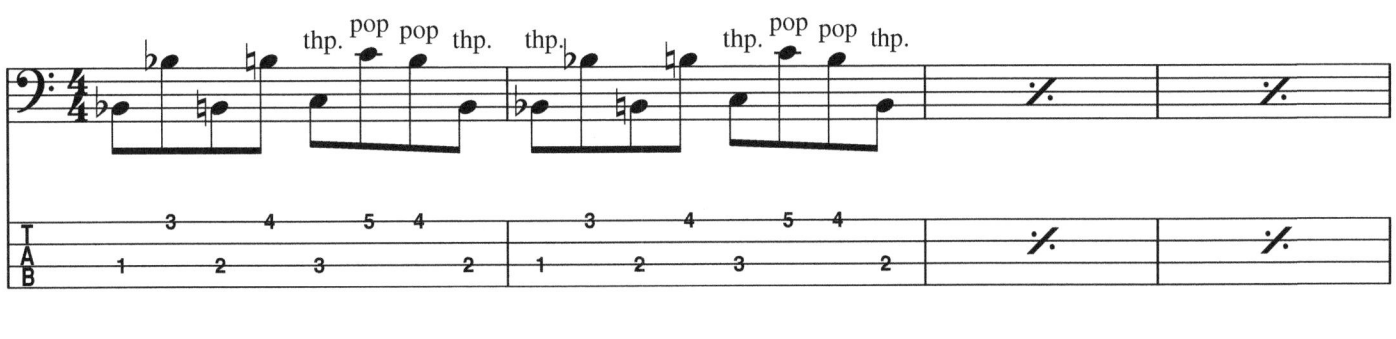

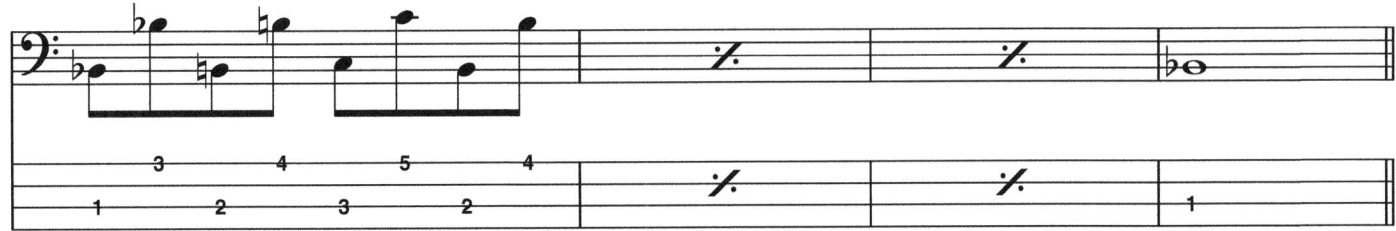

Count! The first pop comes in on the "and" of beat 2.

TRACK 77

Use the same-string thump/pop technique and remember: "thump low, pop high."

TRACK 78

TRACK 79

Try playing all of the grooves on the other strings and even move them around the neck.

Movin' On Up: Playing the 4th, 5th, and 6th Frets

Remember to take your time with the enharmonics in this position. There are two names for most of the notes.

Notes on the G String

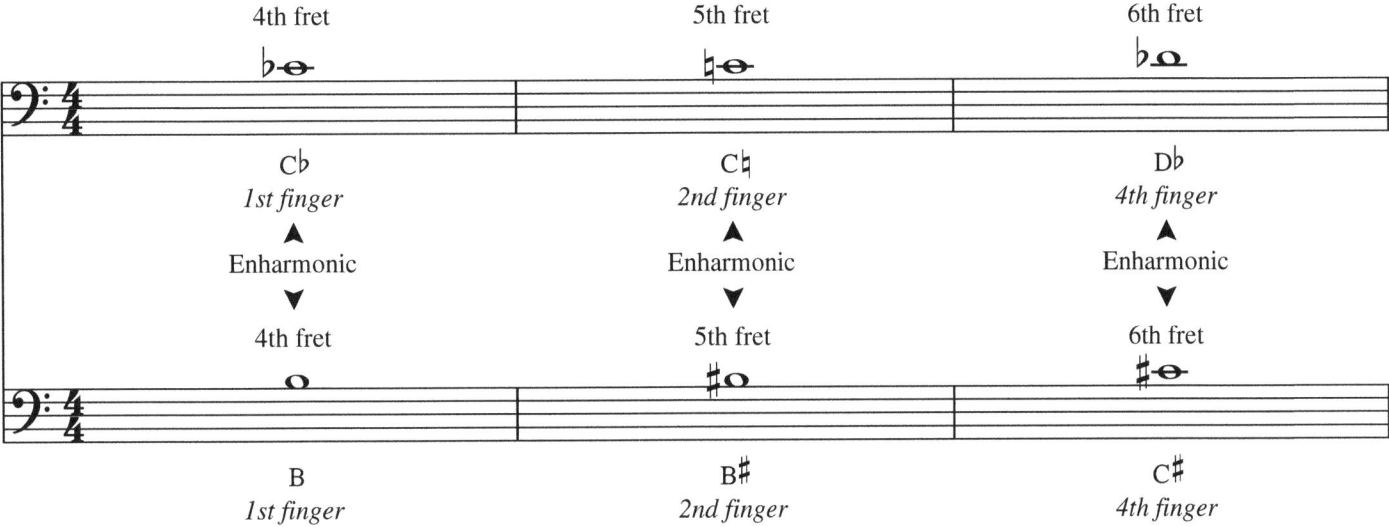

Exercises – G String

TRACK 80

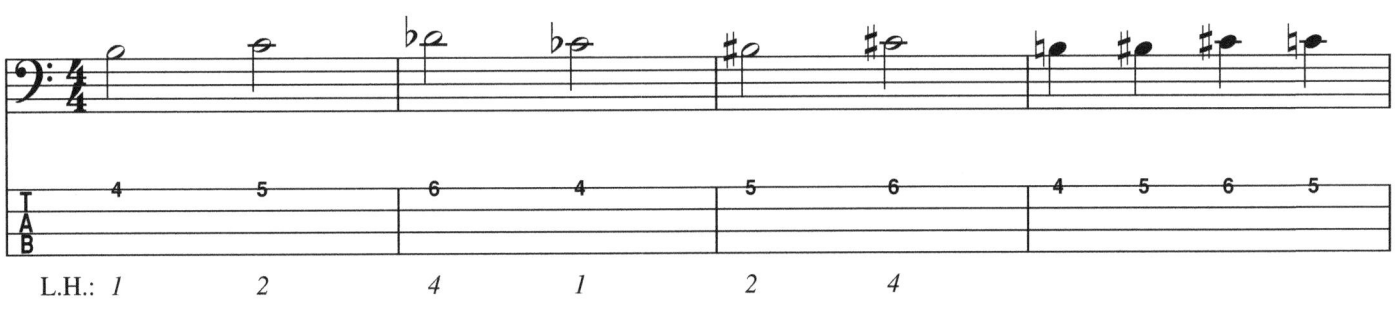

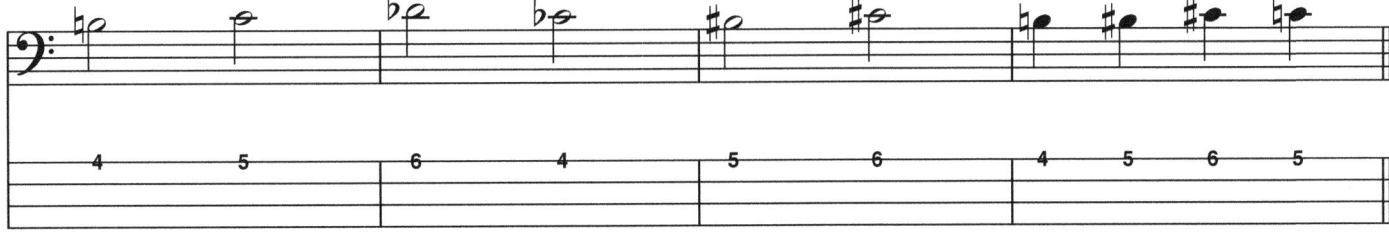

TRACK 81

Notes on the D String

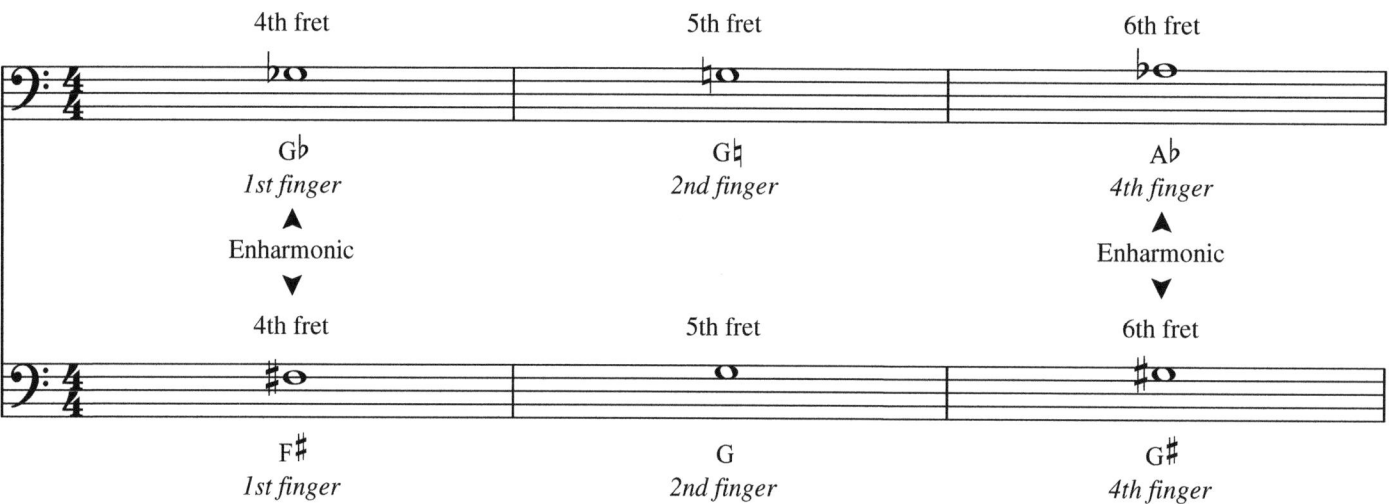

Exercises – D String

TRACK 82

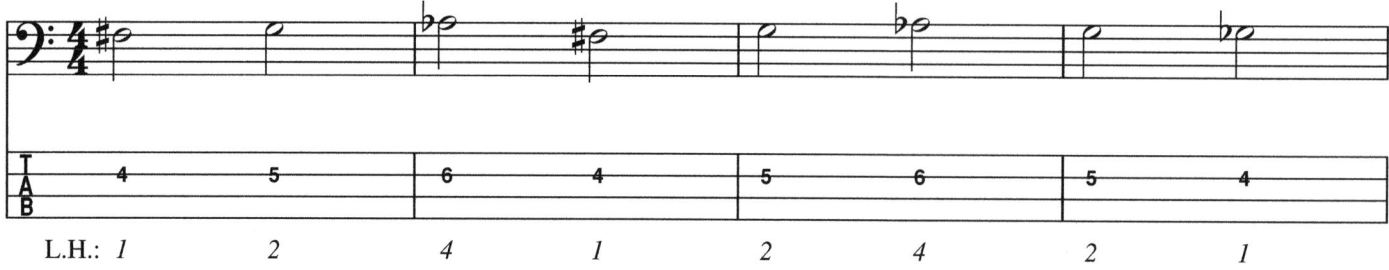

TRACK 83

Notes on the A String

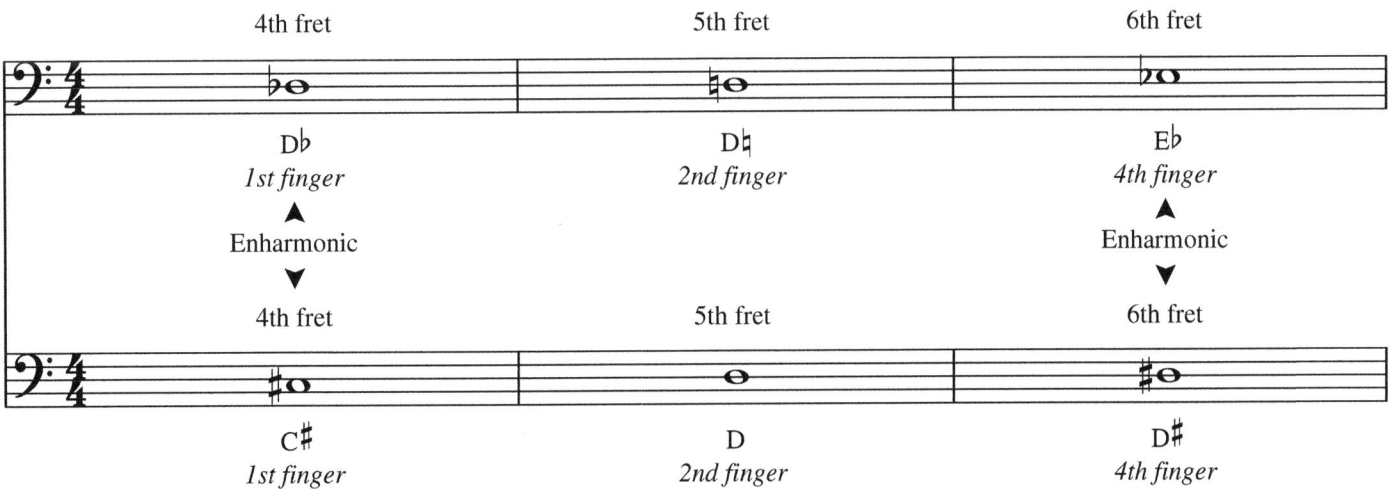

Exercises – A String

TRACK 84

Take this one slowly at first. Be sure to count through the shuffle and triplet rhythms.

TRACK 85

Notes on the E String

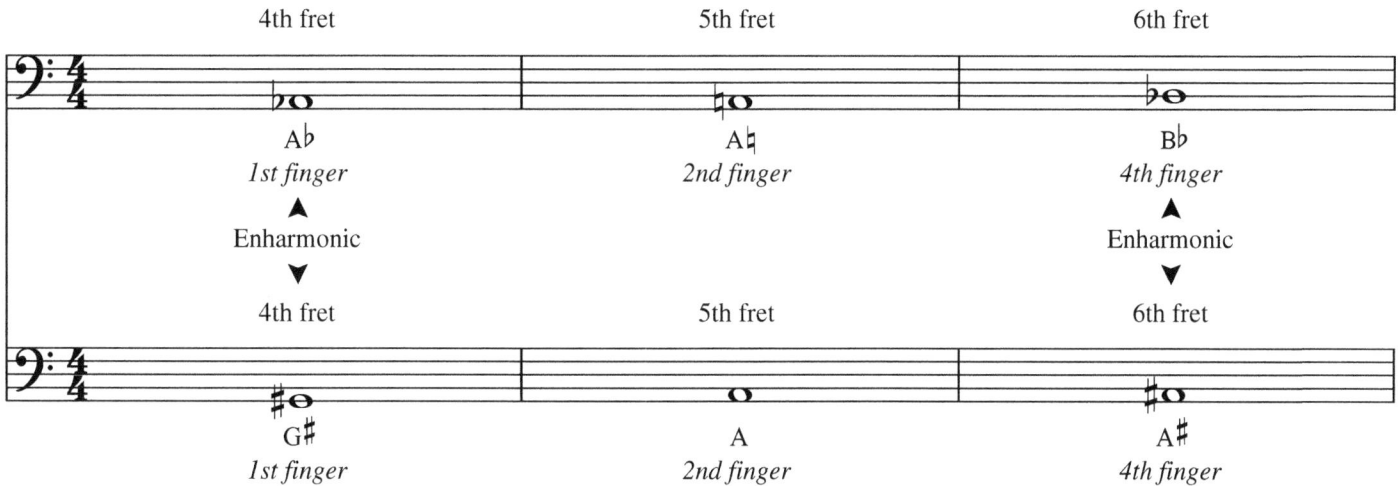

Exercises – E String

Count, count, count!

Playing on All of the Strings

TRACK 88

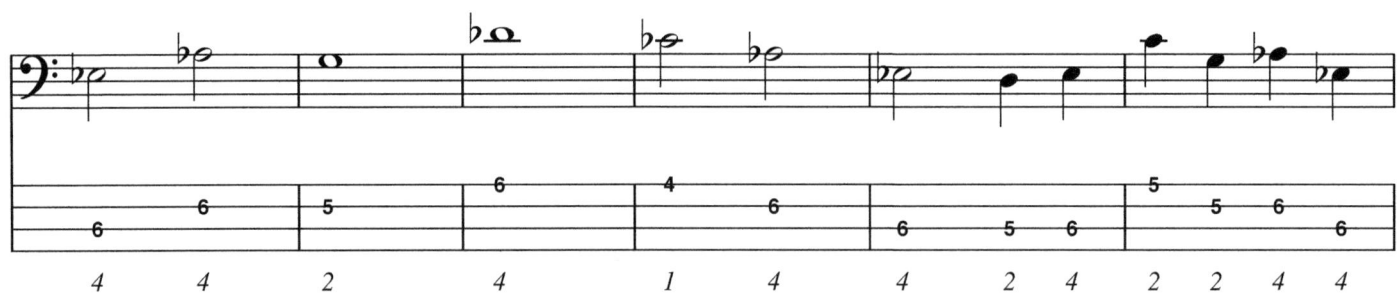

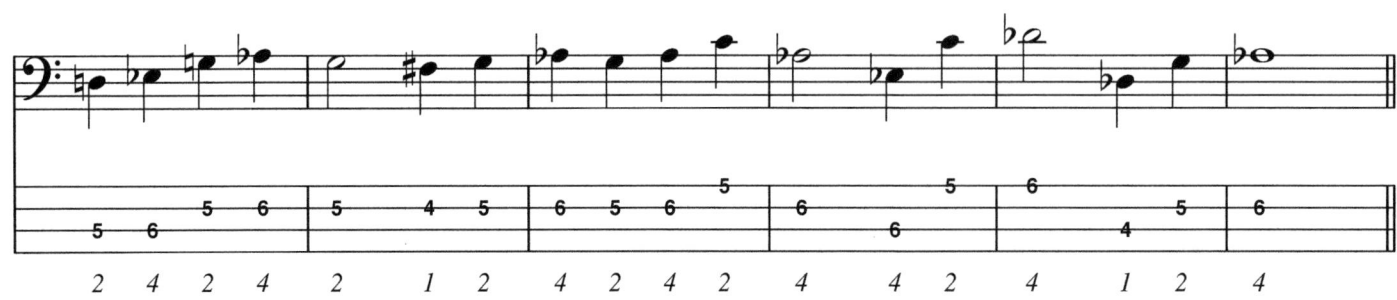

D♭ Major Scale

Practice the D♭ major scale (D♭–E♭–F–G♭–A♭–B♭–C–D♭), shifting through the earlier positions. As you can see by the key signature, there are five flats in the key of D♭. Remember to keep the form of your hand as you shift with your thumb. Try this exercise as whole, half, quarter, and eighth notes.

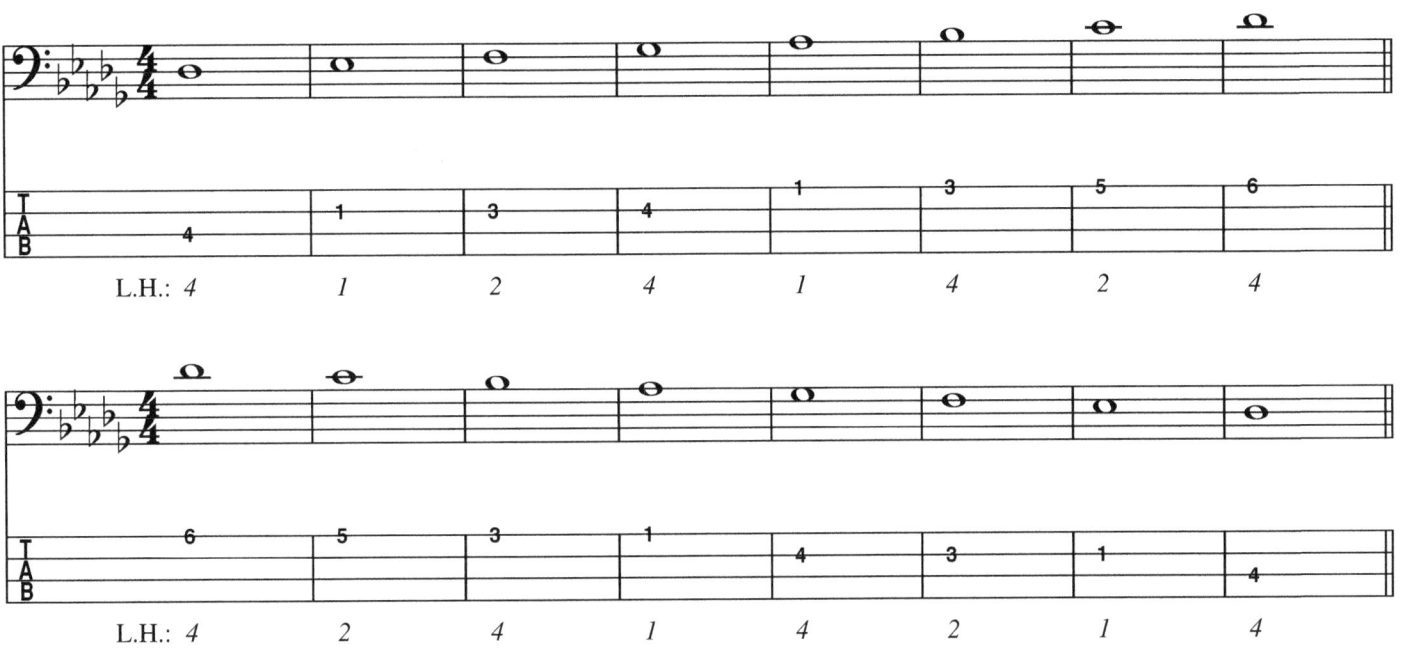

D♭ Major Scale – Alternate Fingering

Here is an alternate fingering that will help minimize movement. Memorize this pattern! As an added bonus, this pattern can be moved around the neck to create a major scale from any starting note. Try it with the C major scale at the 3rd fret and the B major scale at the 2nd fret of the A string.

The shifts are now within one fret of each other. On the strings with three notes, be sure to use all three fingers—index, middle, ring/pinky. This will build strength and dexterity.

Exercise – D♭ Major Scale

TRACK 89

A♭ Major Scale

The A♭ major scale (A♭–B♭–C–D♭–E♭–F–G–A♭) can be played in the same position as the D♭ major scale (3rd position). This pattern will move through all of the earlier positions. Realize that the last two notes (G–A♭) can also be played on the G string.

A♭ Major Scale – Movable Fingering

This fingering is the alternate/movable pattern shown with the D♭ major scale.

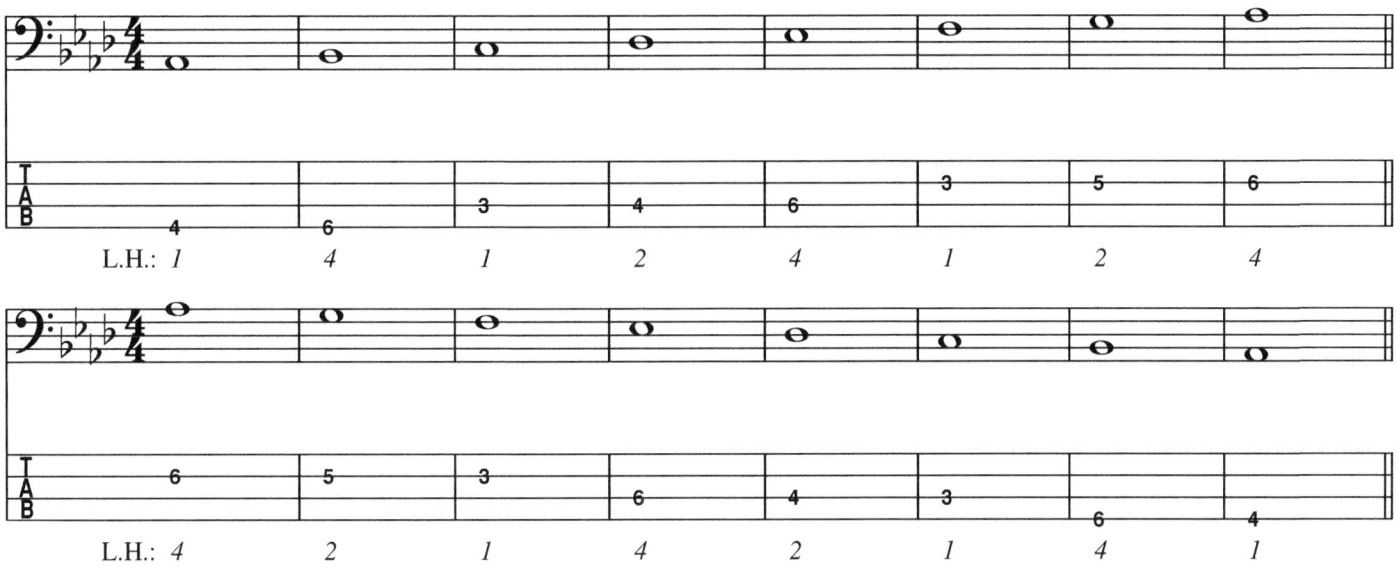

Exercises – A♭ Major Scale

These exercises combine both of the fingerings. While fingerings are given, try to play each exercise with only one of the fingering patterns at a time.

In measure 4, you'll need to shift for the F at the 1st fret.

TRACK 90

In measures 13–14, you'll need to shift again to the 1st fret.

TRACK 91

Challenge yourself—go back to the C major scale exercises or even the song "Jingle Bells" and try to play them with the same movable fingering, instead of using the open strings.

Movin' On Up: Playing the 5th, 6th, and 7th Frets

If you took some time to get to know the landmarks (3rd, 5th, and 7th frets), this position should feel a little familiar.

Notes on the G String

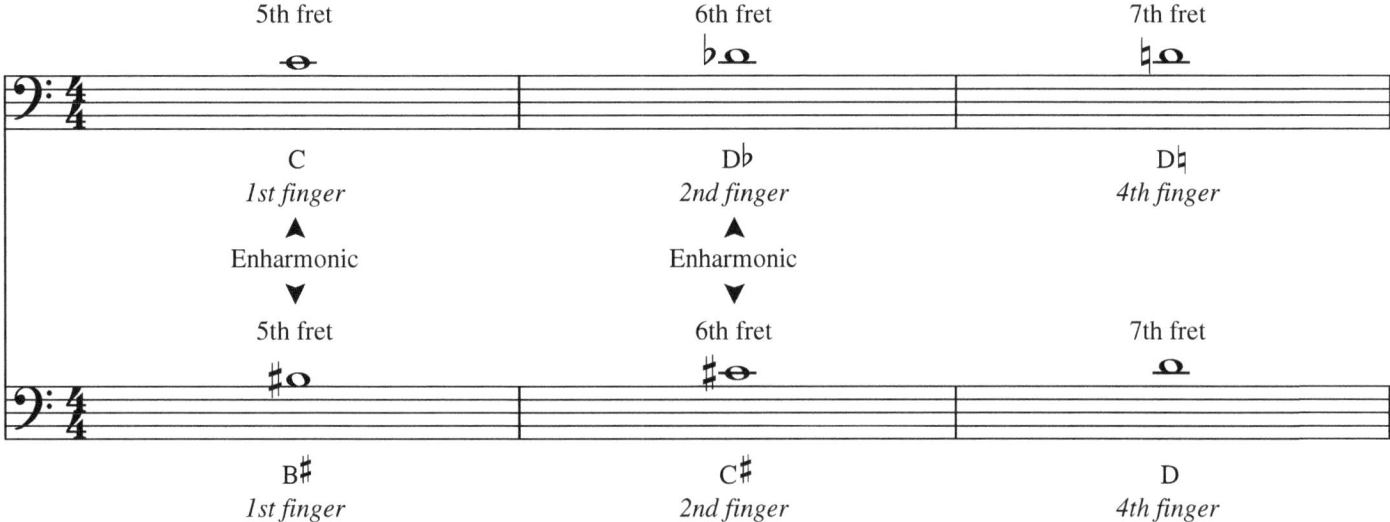

Exercises – G String

TRACK 92

TRACK 93

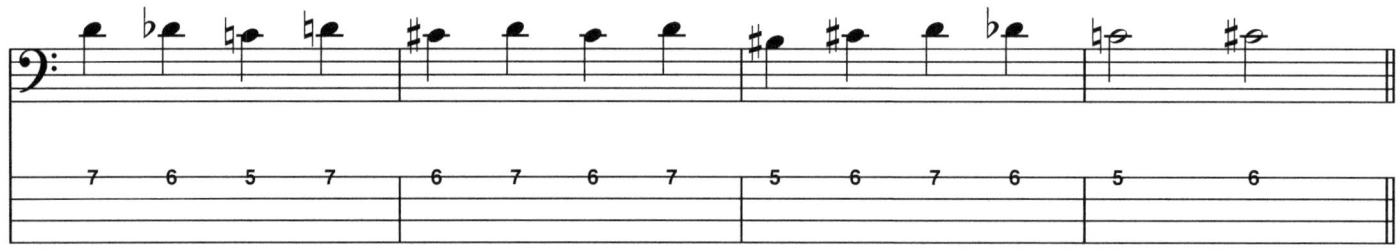

Notes on the D String

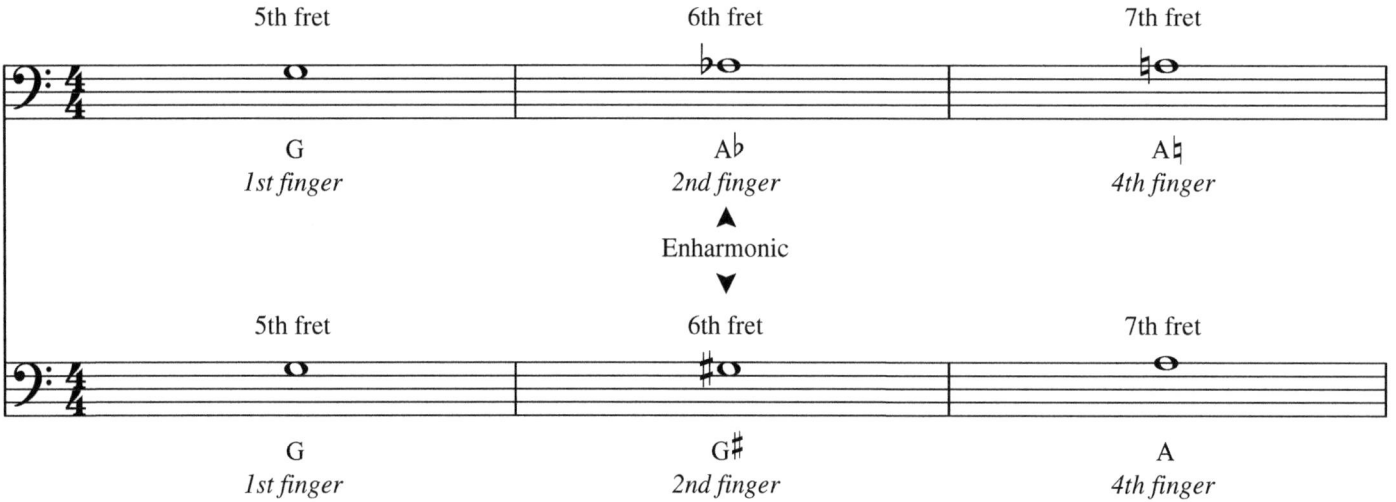

Exercises – D String

TRACK 94

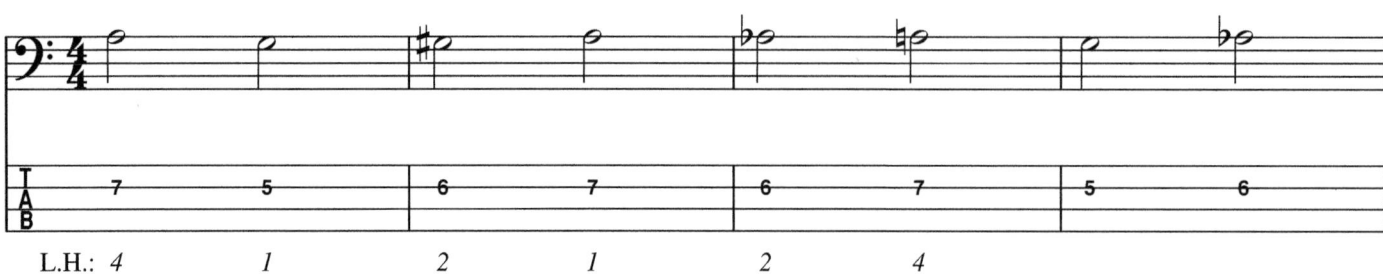

TRACK 95

Notes on the A String

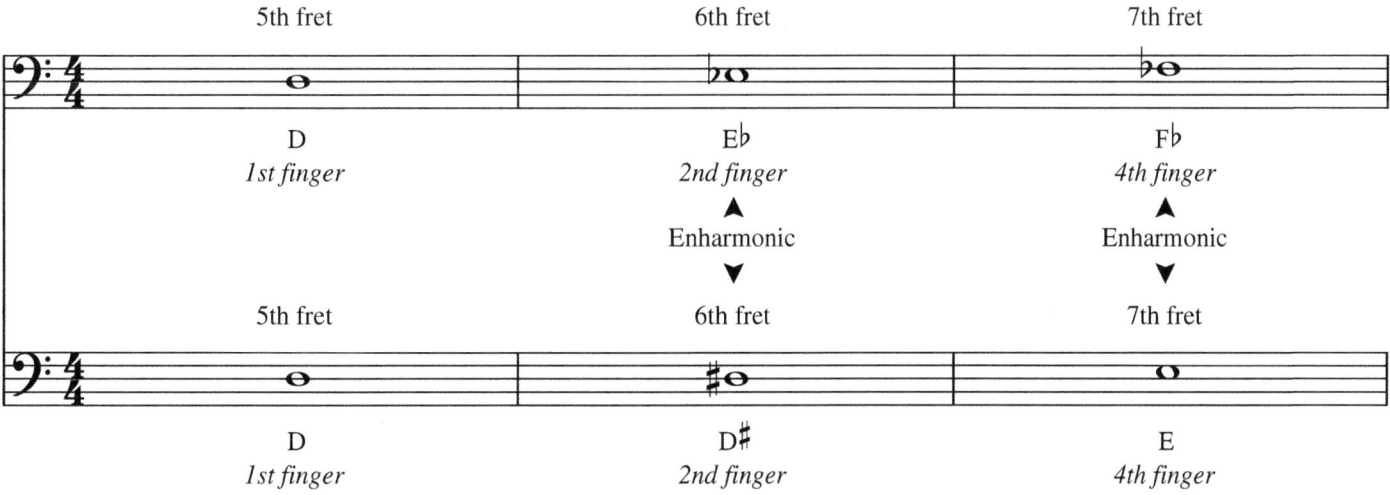

Exercises – A String

TRACK 96

L.H.: 1   2   4   1

TRACK 97

Notes on the E String

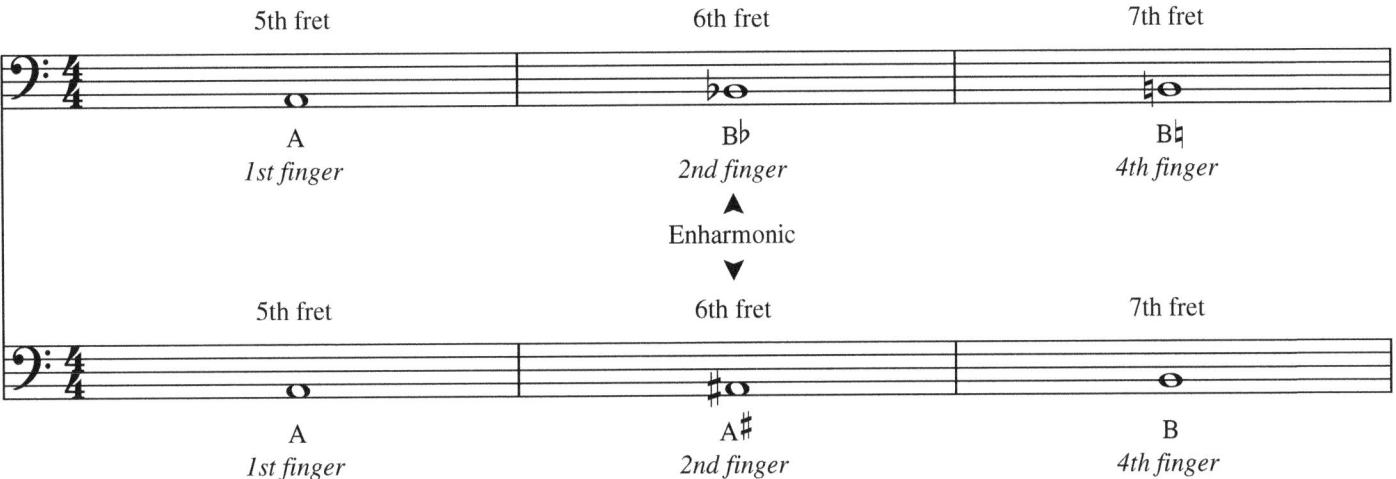

Exercises – E String

TRACK 98

TRACK 99

Playing on All of the Strings

TRACK 100

D Major Scale

There are two sharps in the key of D major (D–E–F#–G–A–B–C#–D). The following fingering moves up the D and G strings.

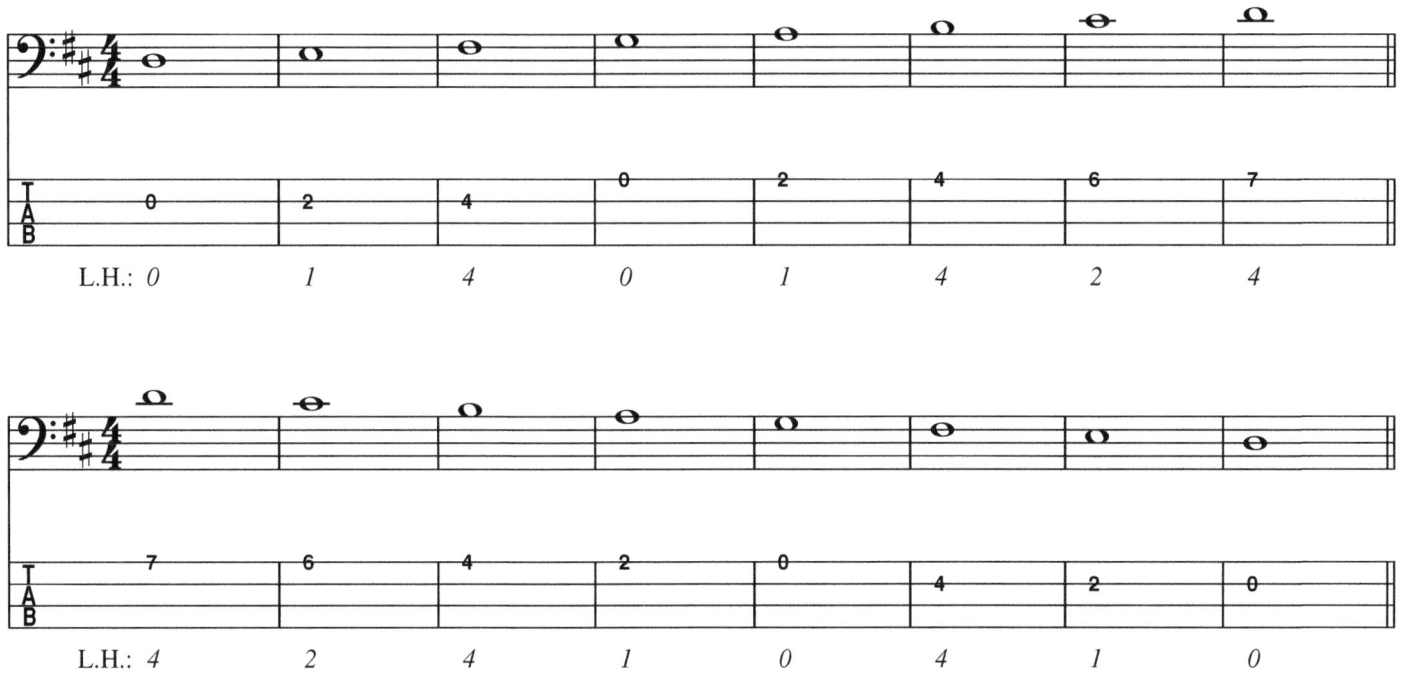

D Major Scale – Movable Fingering

This is the same movable pattern as before. Did you memorize the pattern yet?

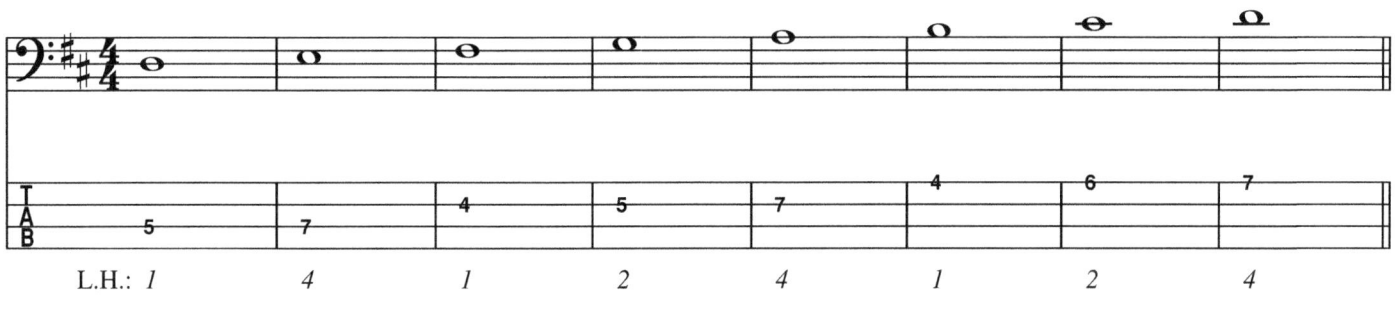

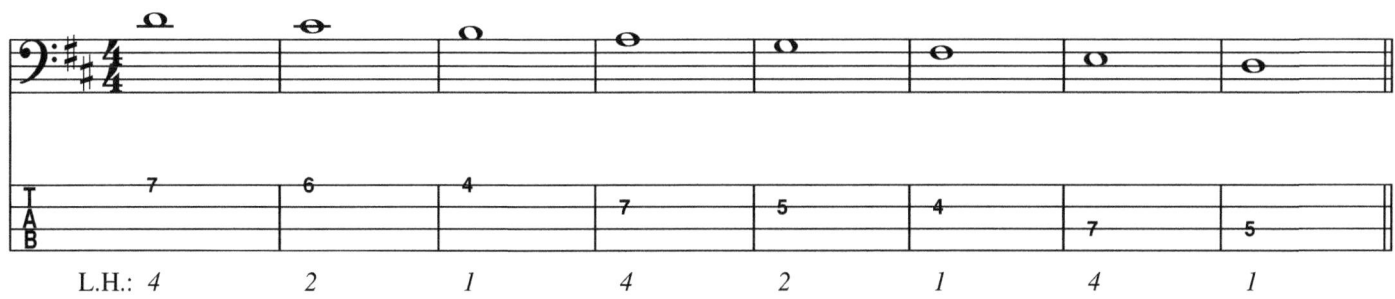

Exercises – D Major Scale

The first exercise is played with the open strings. Play this at the 2nd-fret position as if you were playing the D major scale up the D and G strings.

Notice the word "vamp" at the beginning of these bass grooves. A *vamp* is a section of music that is repeated until cued to move forward. Being able to hold a steady groove through a vamp is an essential skill for any bassist.

TRACK 101

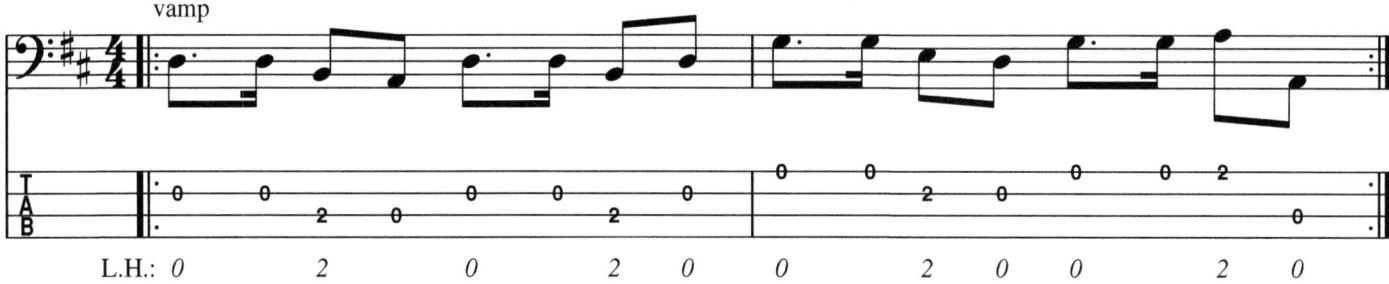

Now play the same groove at the 5th-fret position, using the movable fingerings.

TRACK 102

Movin' On Up: Playing the 6th, 7th, and 8th Frets

Notes on the G String

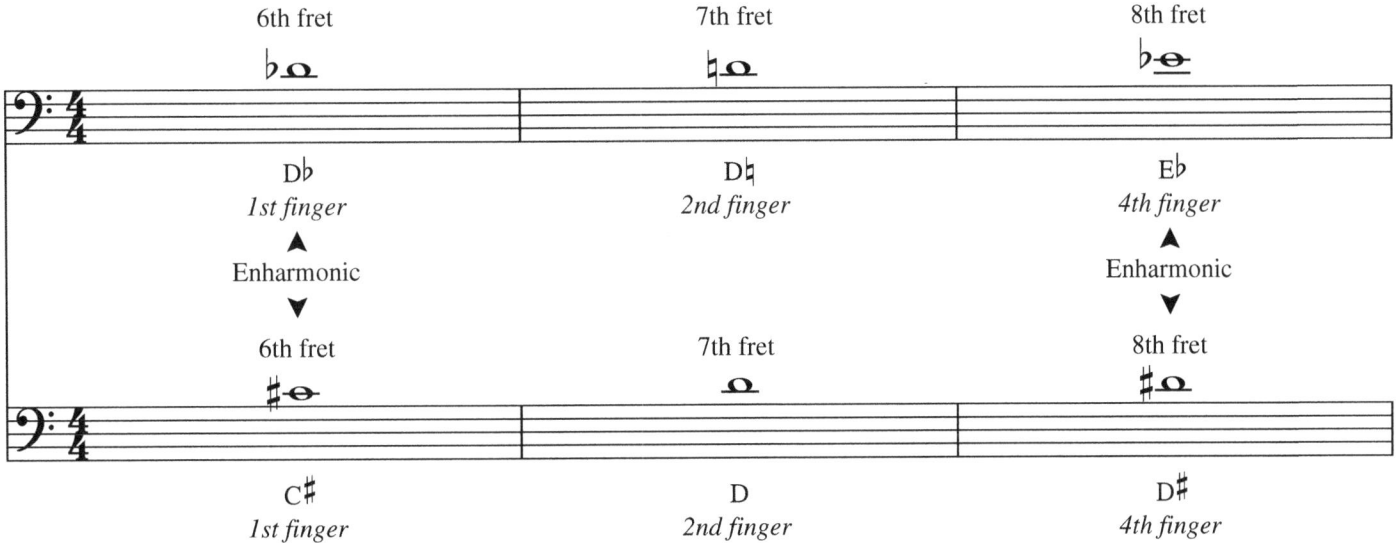

Exercises – G String

TRACK 103

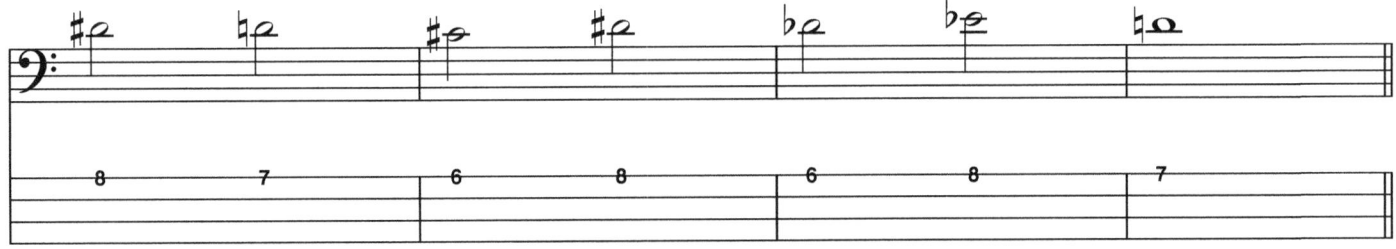

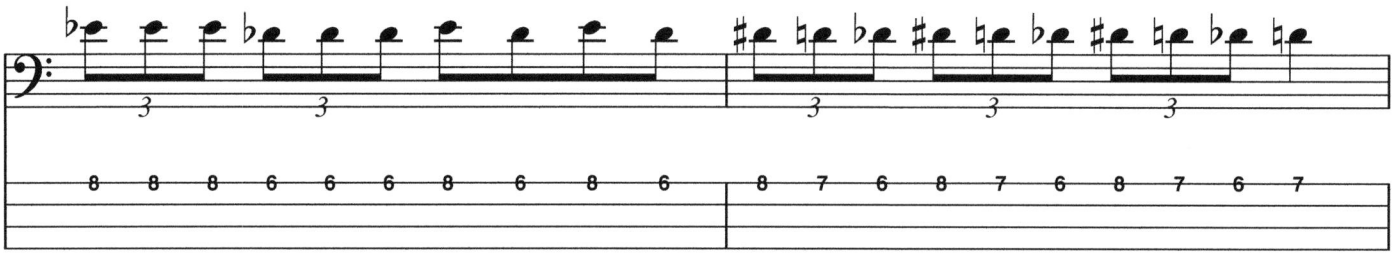

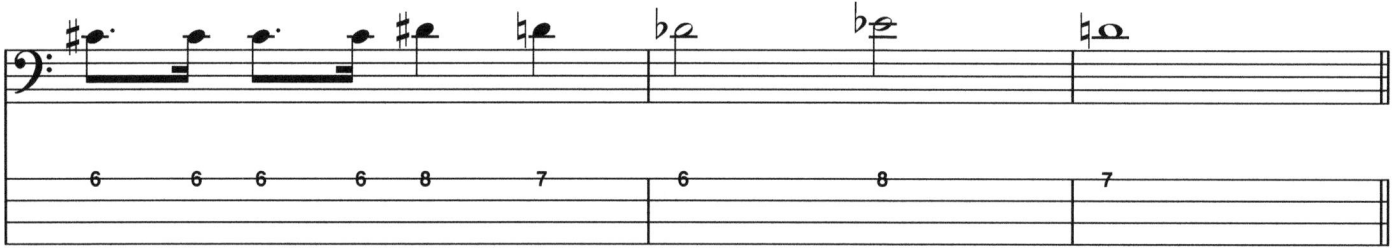

Notes on the D String

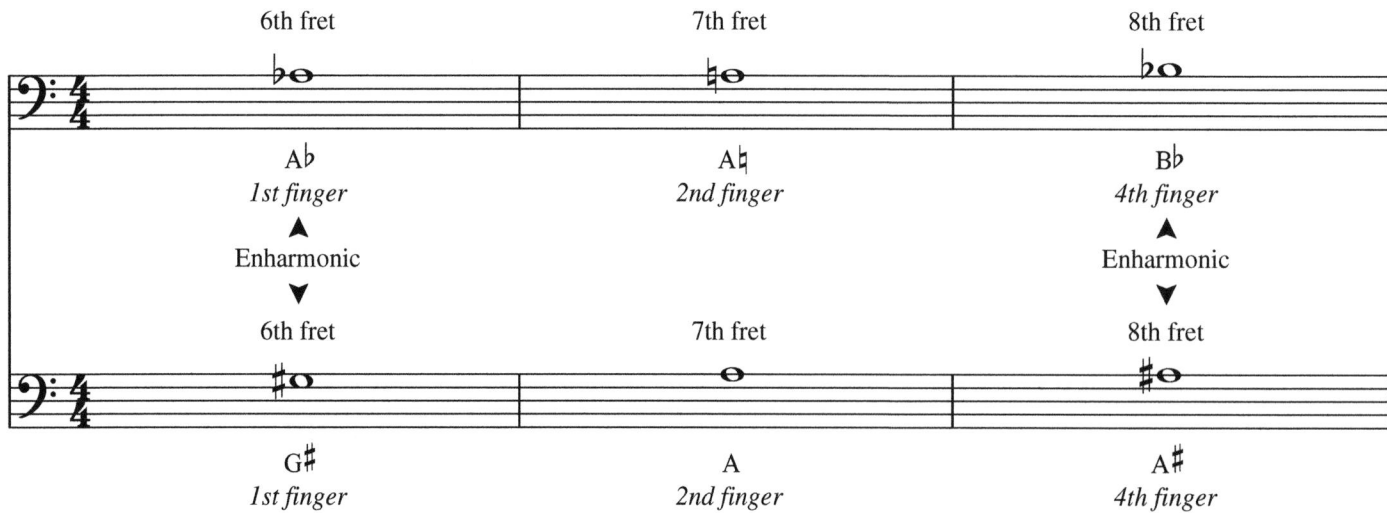

Exercises – D String

TRACK 105

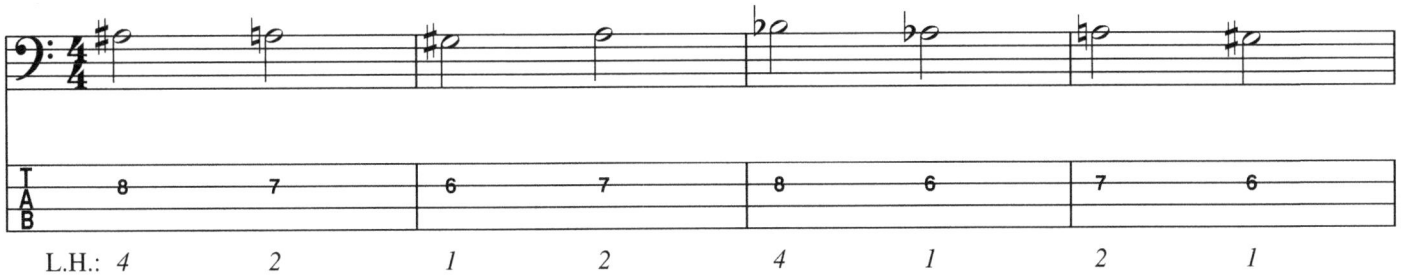

TRACK 106

Notes on the A String

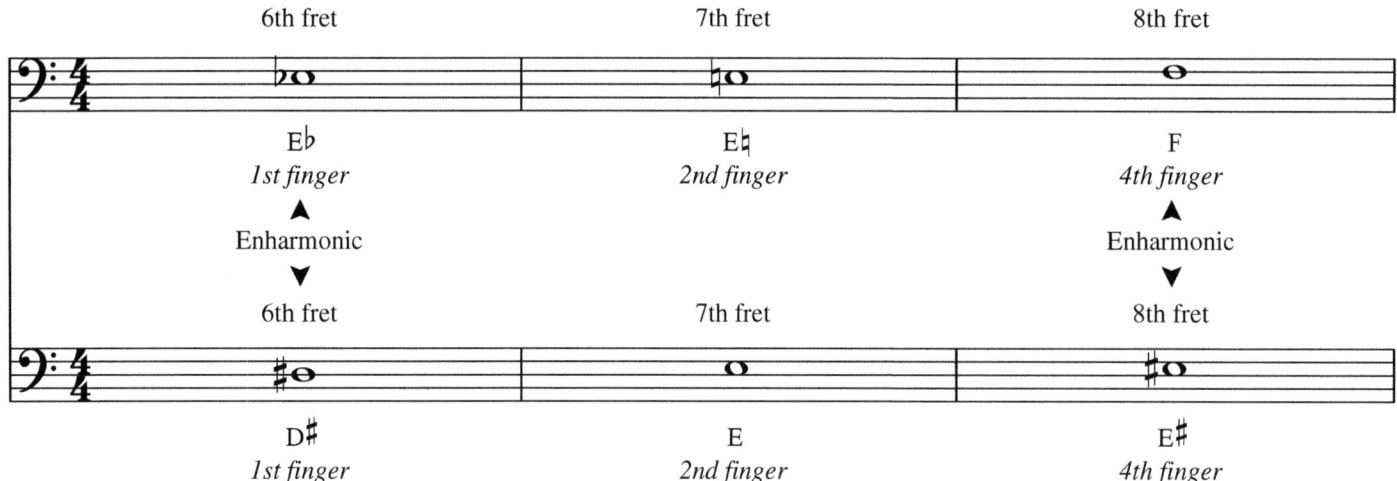

Exercises – A String

There are rests and 16th note rhythms in these exercises. Remember, there are four evenly spaced 16th notes in one quarter note. Use the syllables "1–e–and–a" to count out the beat.

TRACK 107

TRACK 108

Notes on the E String

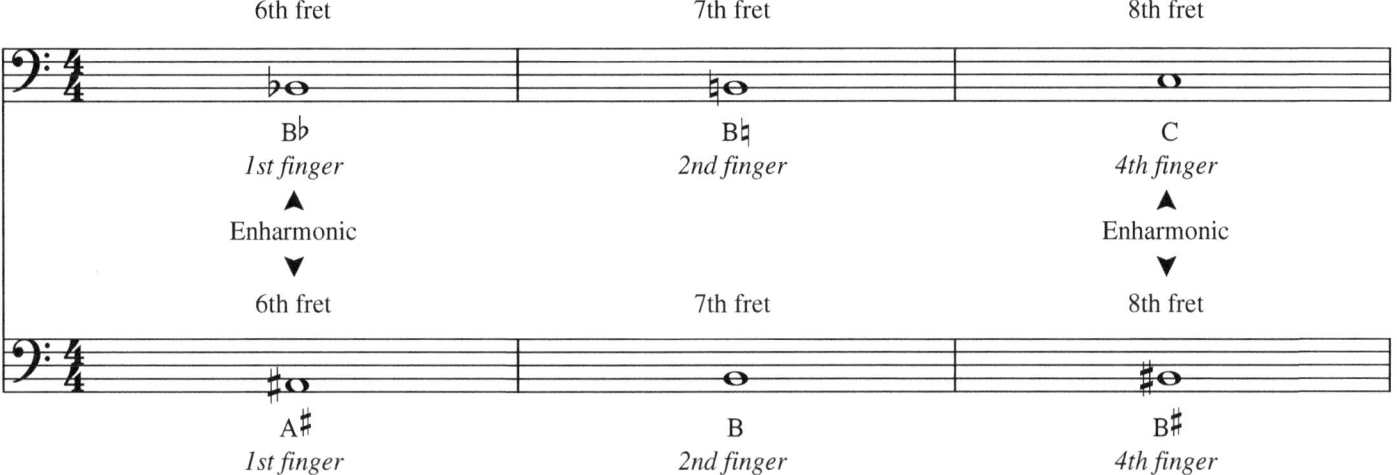

Exercises – E String

Be sure to count through this one. In measures 5–9, beat 1 contains 16th notes and beat 2 contains triplets.

TRACK 109

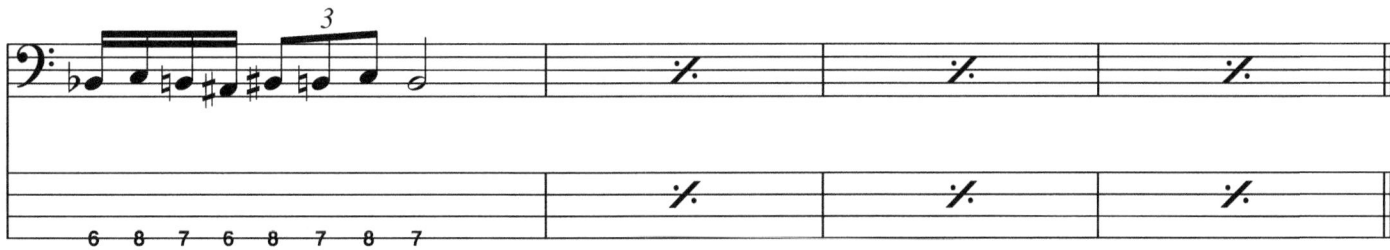

TRACK 110

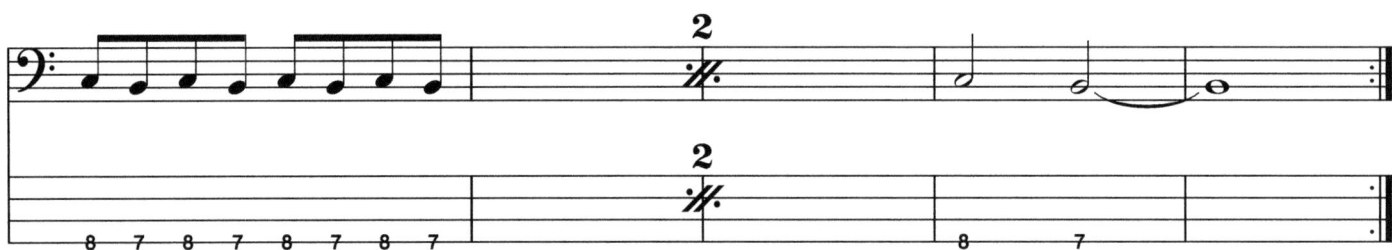

Playing on All of the Strings

While this one is rhythmically simple, take your time with the enharmonics on each string.

TRACK 111

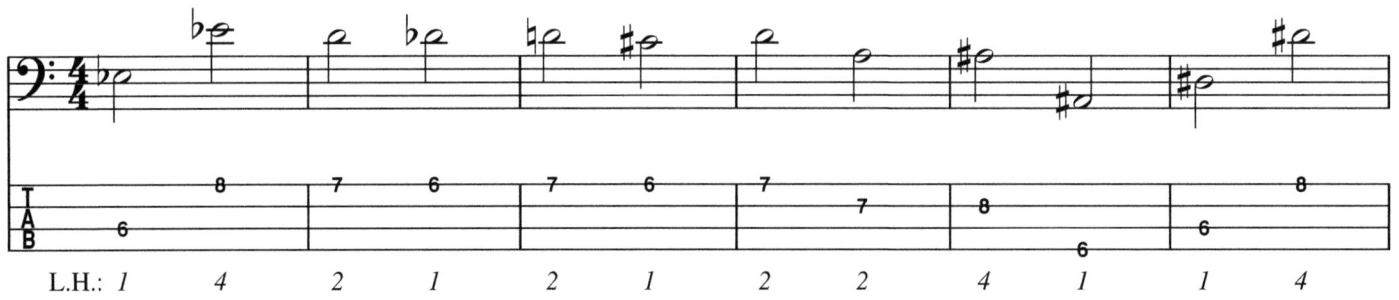

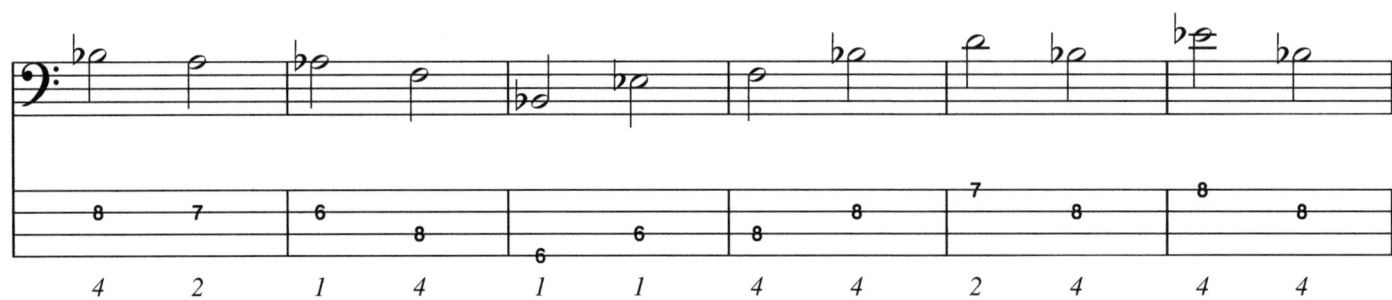

E♭ Major Scale

There are three flats in the key of E♭ major (E♭–F–G–A♭–B♭–C–D–E♭). This fingering will move up the D and G strings—similar to the D major scale fingering.

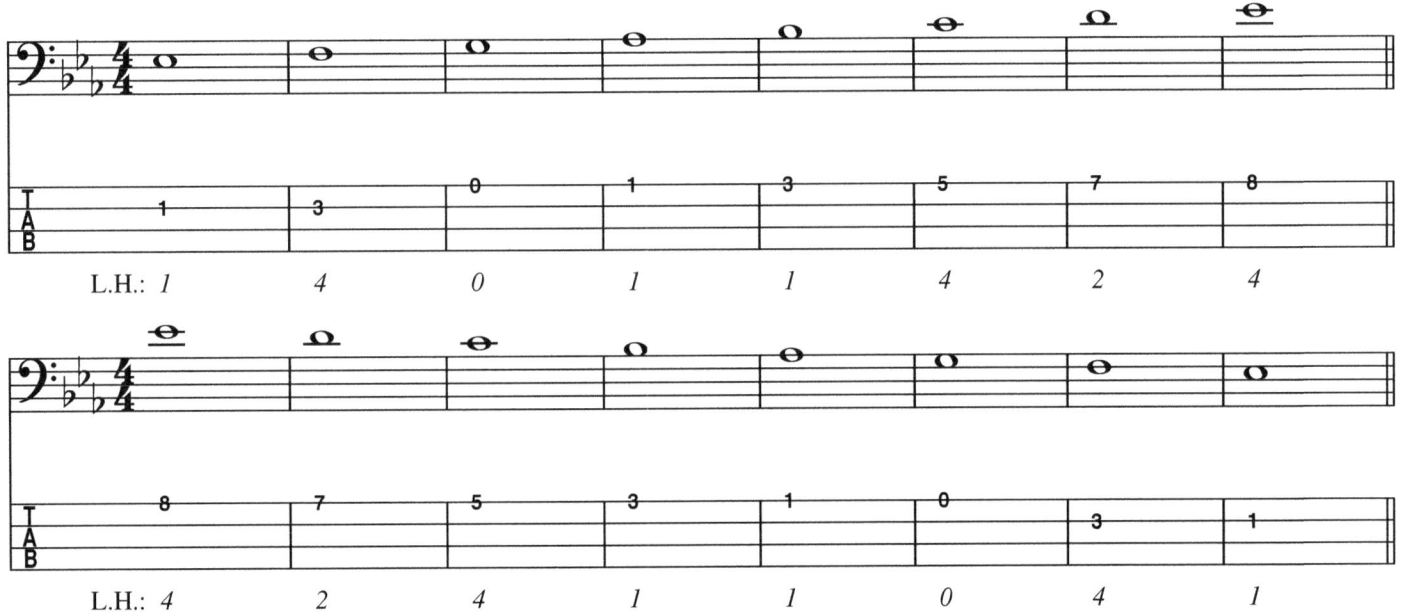

E♭ Major Scale – Movable Fingering

You guessed it—played across the strings at the 6th-fret position.

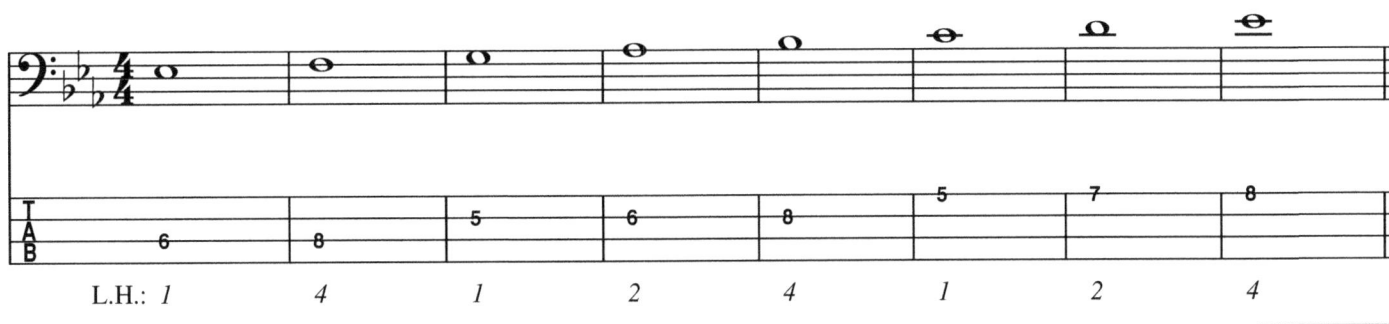

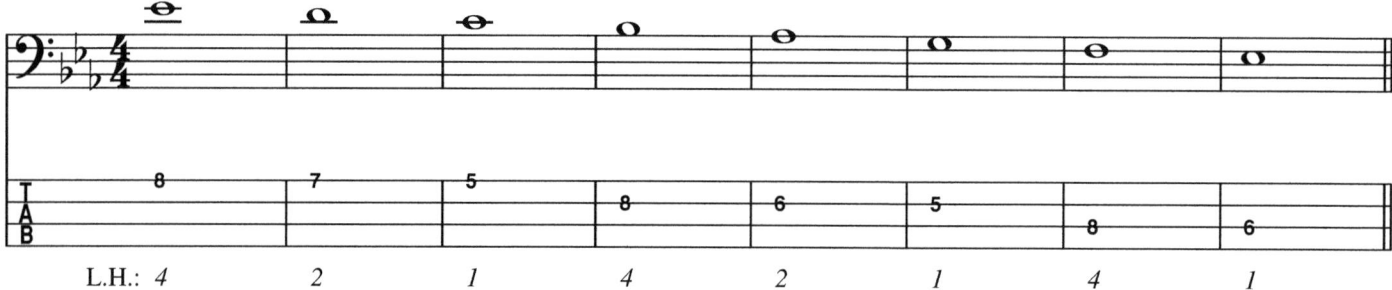

Exercise – E♭ Major Scale

This is a typical walking bass line. It combines both of the major-scale fingerings and moves throughout all of the positions covered so far. Play the exercise with the given fingerings. Shift with your 1st finger between the A♭ and B♭ on the G string. Be sure to keep a steady quarter-note rhythm as you walk through the music.

TRACK 112

Syncopation

Syncopation is the accenting of beats that are not usually accented. For example, think about tapping your foot while counting eighth notes: "1–and, 2–and, 3–and, 4–and." The number—or *downbeat*—is the strong beat, and the "and" is the weak beat, or *upbeat.* By accenting notes on the upbeat, the feel becomes syncopated.

Phrase Markings

Phrase markings can be added to notes to emphasize how they are played. There are many markings. Three of the most common are the *staccato, accent,* and *fermata* markings.

A dot above or below the note is a staccato mark (♩). Don't confuse this marking with the rhythmic notation of the dotted note, *where the dot is to the right of the note head.* Play a staccato note by cutting the note short. You can consider playing half of the value of the note.

An inverted "V" over a note is a heavy accent mark (♩). Accented notes are stressed when played—or played with extra force so that they stand out.

A fermata holds the note until cued to end (or to move on). This mark commonly is placed over the last note of a song or phrase (𝄐).

Exercises

Begin by playing through the following exercises without the phrase markings. Add the markings only after you are comfortable with each exercise.

The first two exercises are in the key of E♭. They have a similar feel, even though they are written differently.

TRACK 113

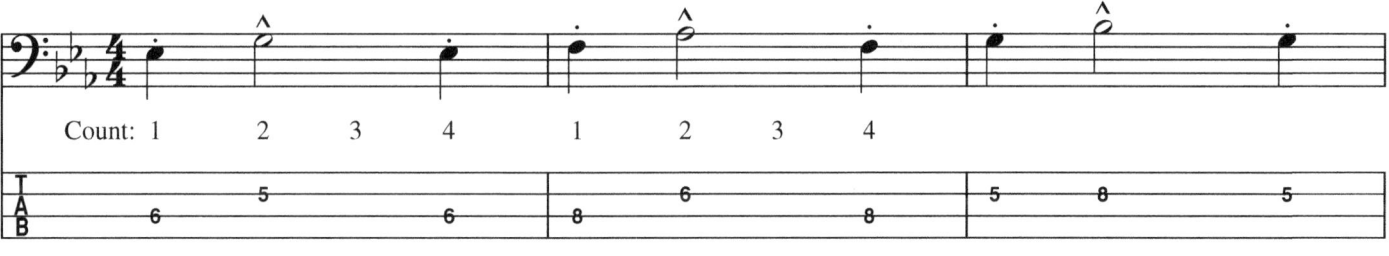

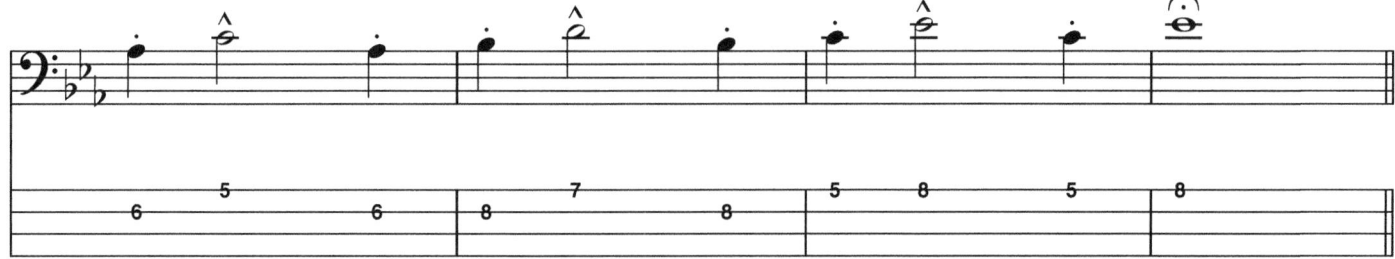

107

This exercise is in 2/4 time—there are only two quarter notes in each bar.

TRACK 114

This exercise is in 3/4 time—there are three quarter notes in each bar. Notice that most of the notes are played on the upbeat (on the "and" of each beat).

TRACK 115

This exercise is in 4/4 time and the key of F. Play this at the 1st-fret position.

TRACK 116

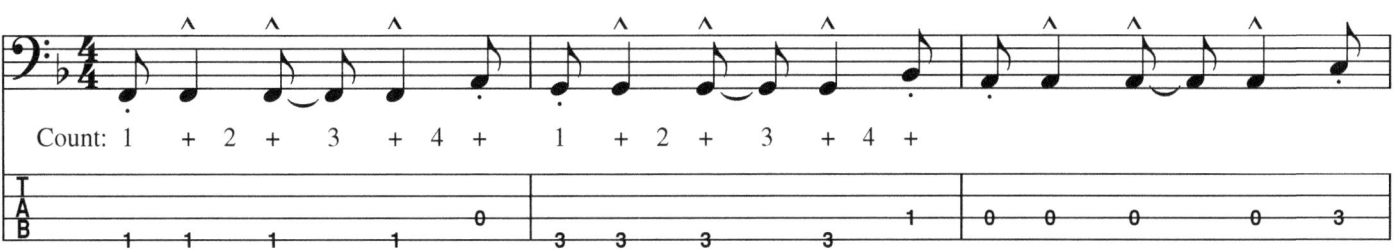

Let's turn the last example into a bass-line groove. In measures 5–6, use your 1st finger for the low notes and your 4th finger for the high notes of the octave pattern.

TRACK 117

Movin' On Up: Playing the 7th, 8th, and 9th Frets

Notes on the G String

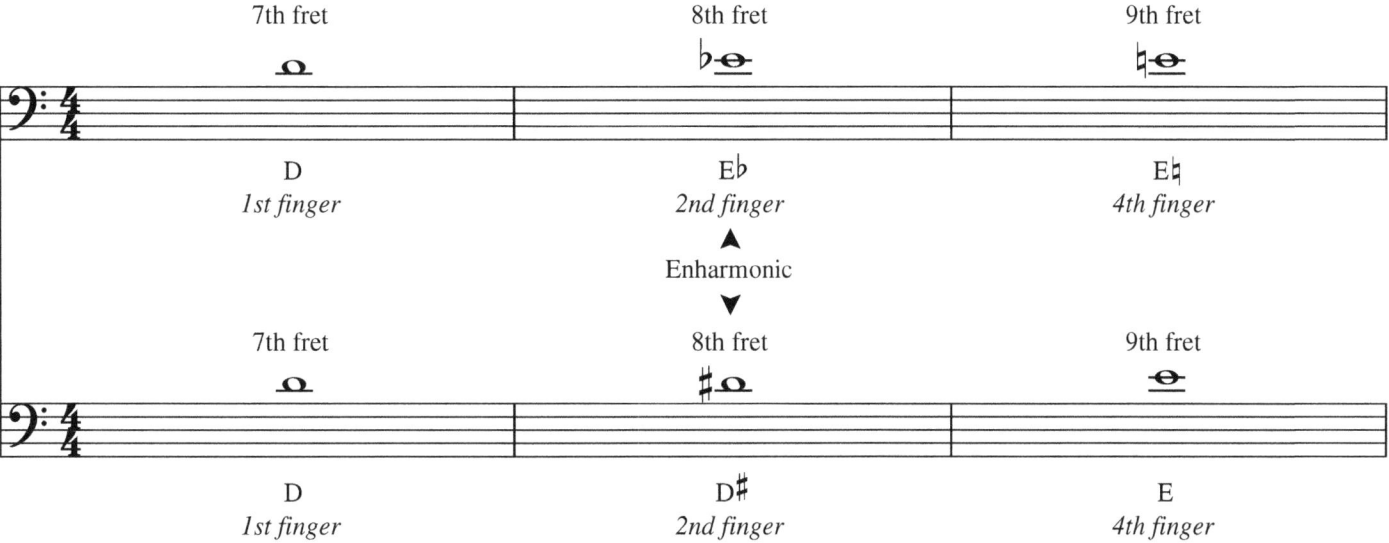

Exercises – G String

Be sure to count the 16th-note patterns: "1–e–and–a, 2–e–and–a, 3–e–and–a, 4–e–and–a."

TRACK 118

TRACK 119

Notes on the D String

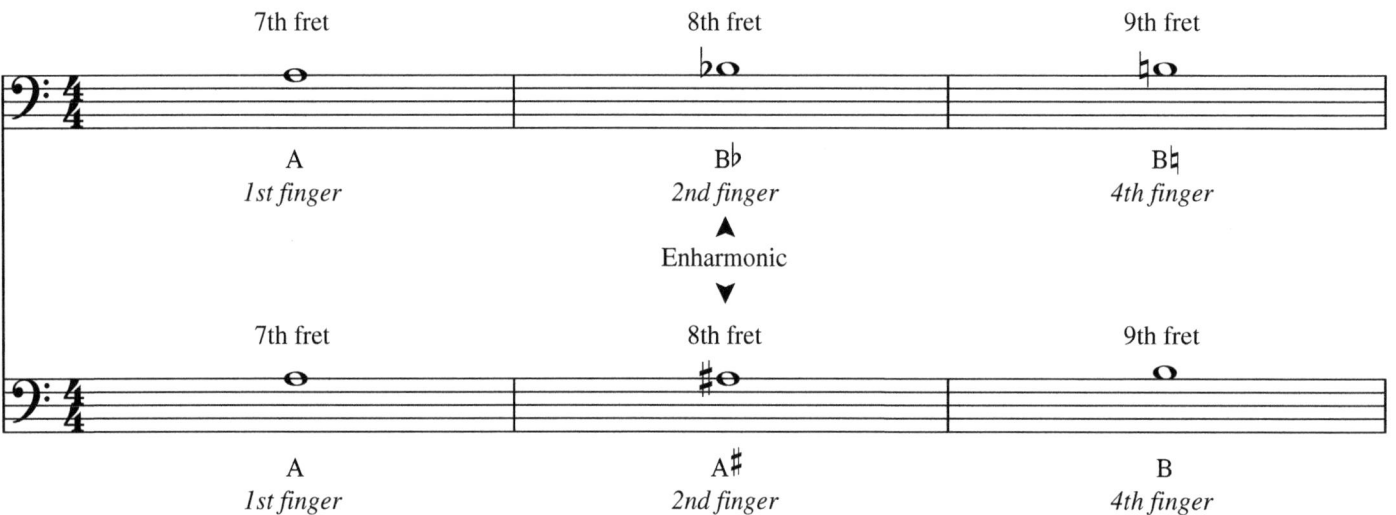

Exercises – D String

TRACK 120

L.H.: 1 2 4 1 2 4 2 4

TRACK 121

Notes on the A String

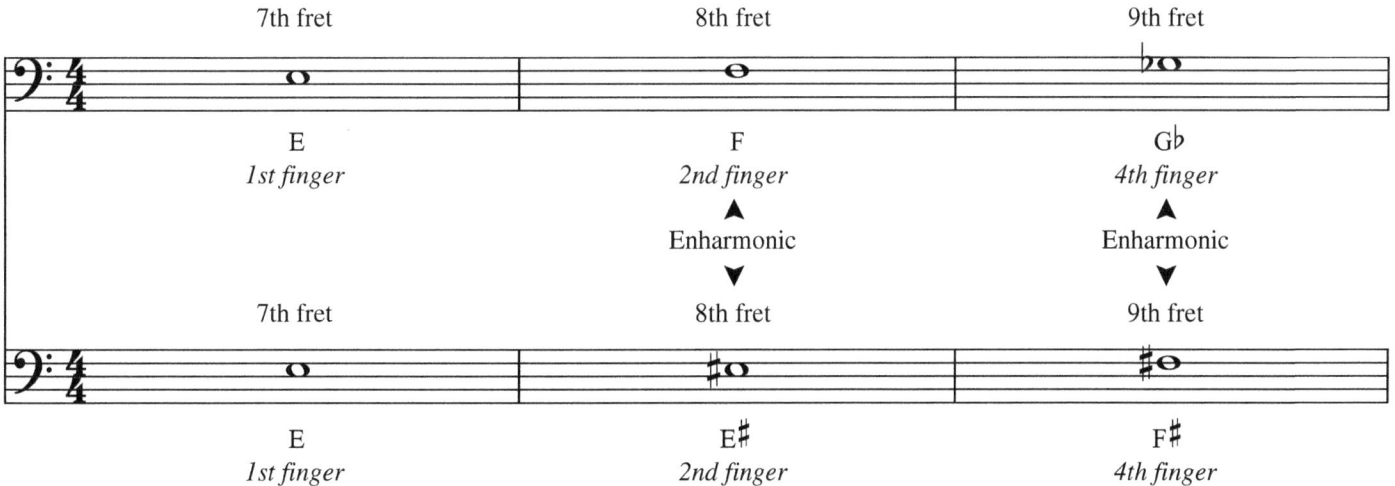

Exercises – A String

These next examples contain some syncopation; be sure to count.

TRACK 122

TRACK 123

Notes on the E String

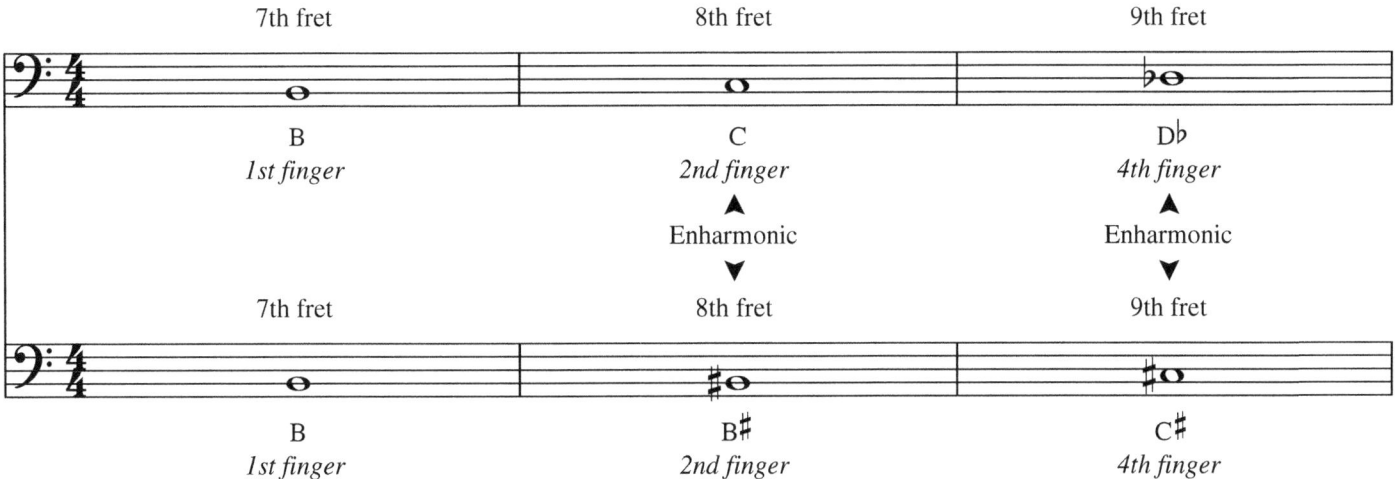

Exercises – E String

Practice these exercises slowly but challenge yourself to see how fast you can *properly* play them.

TRACK 124

TRACK 125

Playing on All of the Strings

TRACK 126

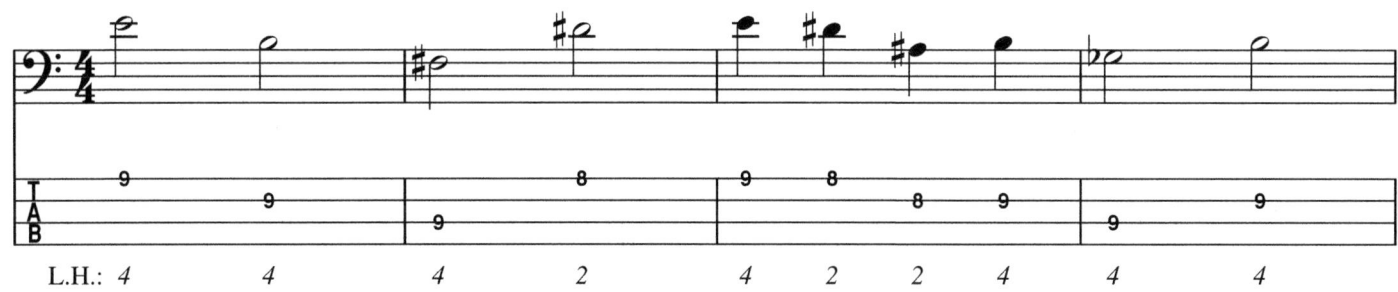

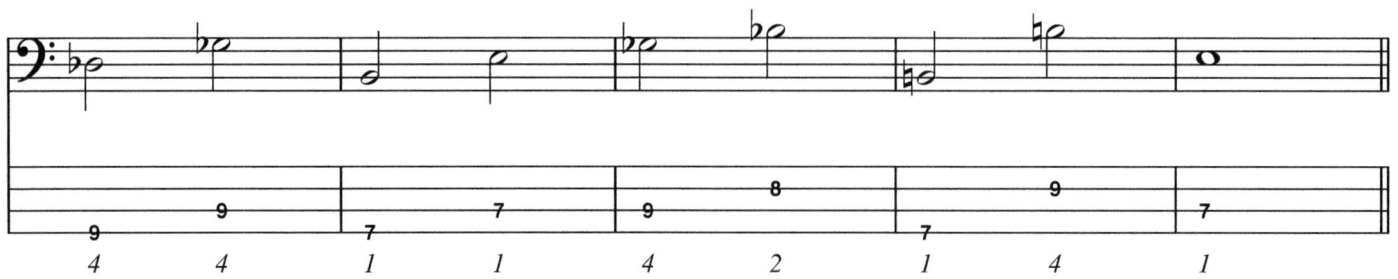

Two-Octave E Major Scale

There are four sharps in E major (E–F#–G#–A–B–C#–D#–E). The following fingering combines both position shifts and the movable pattern to create a two-octave major scale. The asterisk marks the beginning of the second octave, as well as the beginning of the movable fingering pattern.

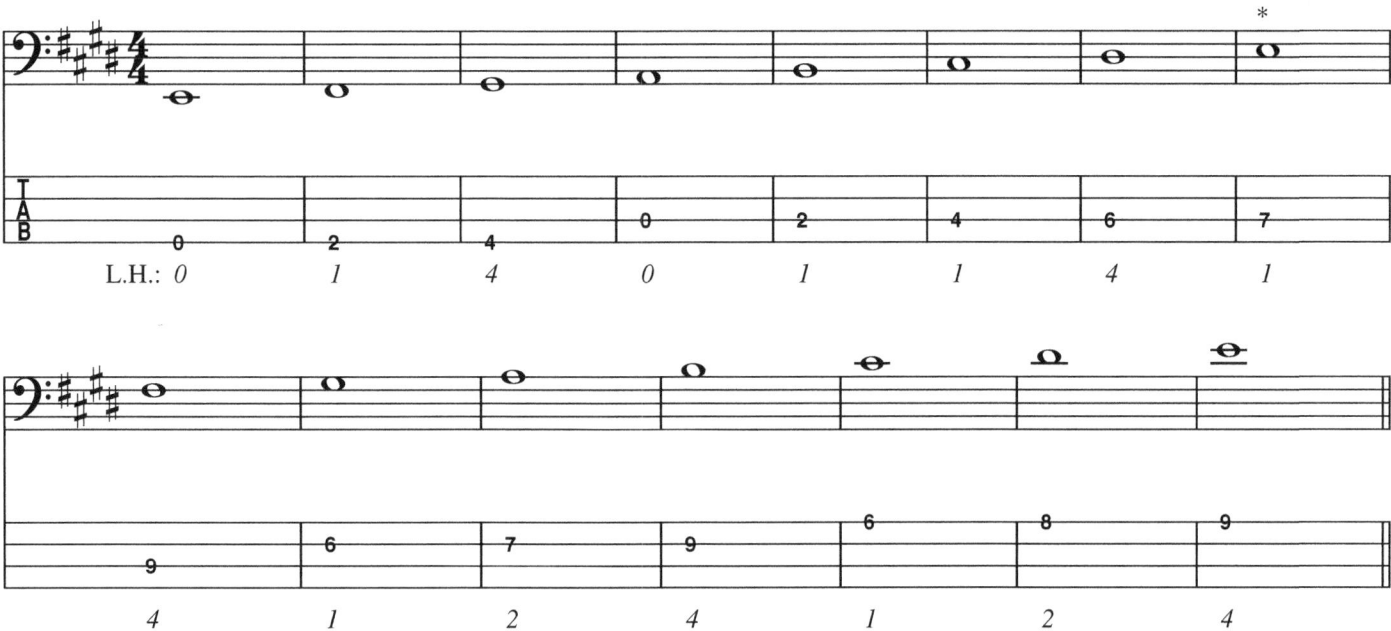

Exercise – E Major Scale

This exercise uses the two-octave E major scale to move through all of the neck positions covered in the book. The asterisk marks a *shift on the same string*.

TRACK 127

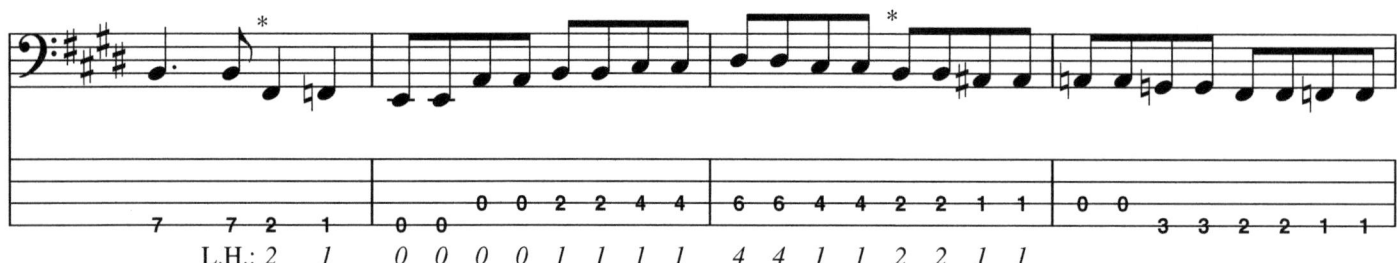

Blues Vamp

Create your own song from this groove. Try to play the same pattern, but starting on the A string!

TRACK 128

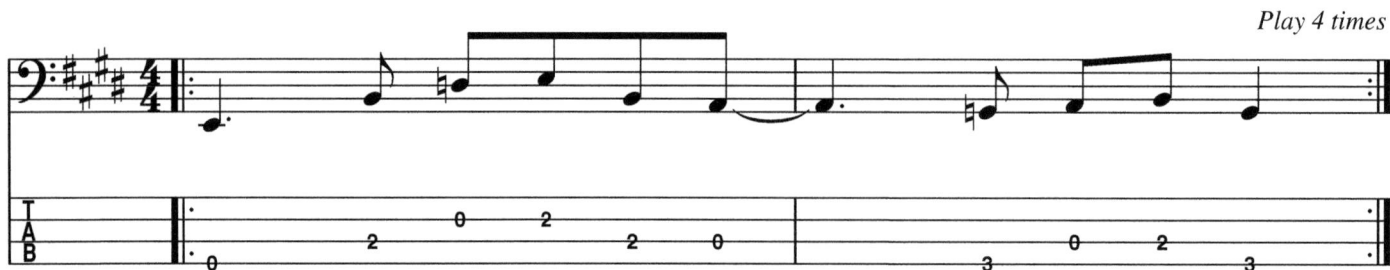

Additional Basic Slappin' Techniques

In addition to the basic slappin' techniques, we're going to be looking at various *double-thump* and *slide* grooves.

The Double-Thump

The double-thump is an essential technique to master—simply thump twice! It's very percussive and anchors the groove.

The first example is going to require the earlier octave technique; use your 1st finger for the lower notes and your 4th finger for the upper octave notes. Here again, in your right hand, thump the low notes and pop the upper notes. The double-thump appears on beat 4. This example starts with a pickup (incomplete bar) on the "and" of beat 4, and it will be held over to beat 1 every time.

TRACK 129

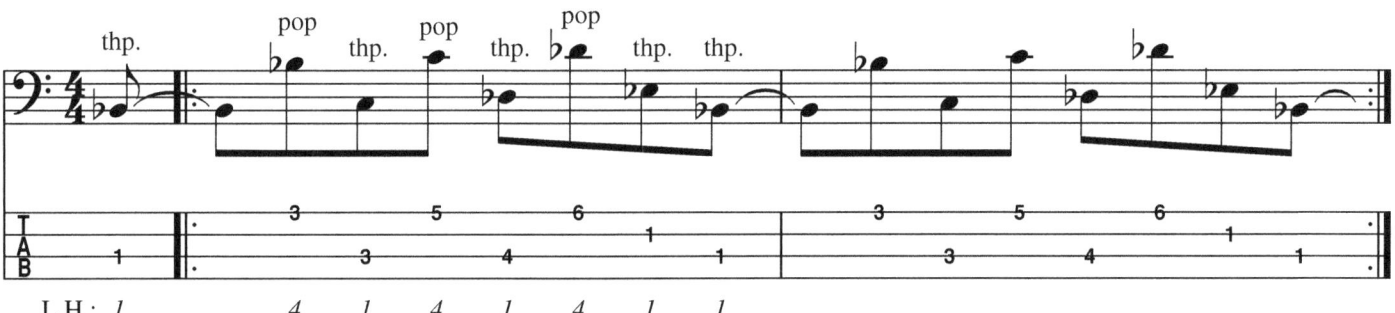

Here the double-thump is right on the downbeat of beats 1 and 3. Use the same octave technique as before. This is a great one with which to build your own bass line—just play the double-thump and pop the octaves on the root of any chord.

TRACK 130

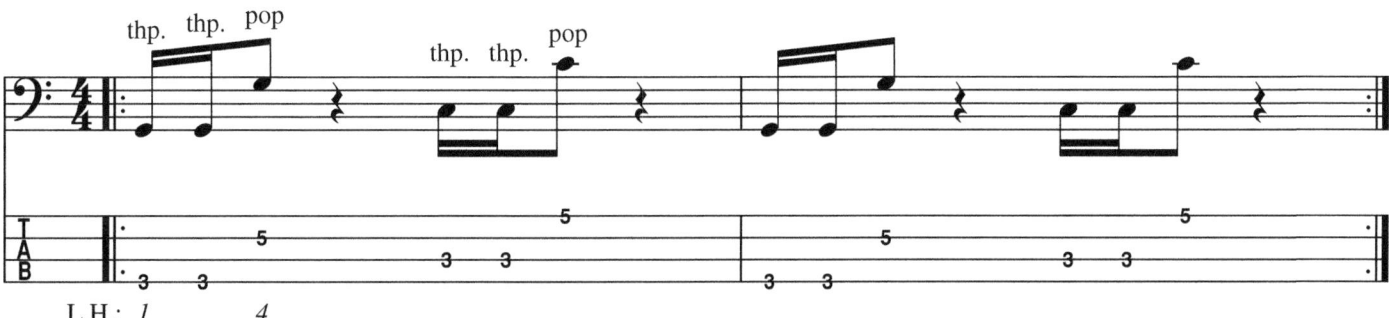

Double-Thumpin' with Shifts

This example utilizes not only the double-thump and octaves, but also the shuffle rhythm, hammer-ons, and shifts, as well. Before tackling this one, look at the notes that you're about to play. All of the low notes are E, the middle notes on the A string are D–E hammer-ons, and the upper notes on the G string also are D–E hammer-ons.

Since the open E string doesn't need to be fretted, keep your hand around the 5th-fret position. This will enable you to quickly shift between the 5th fret of the A string and 7th fret of the G string with your 1st finger. Start all of the hammer-ons with your 1st finger (for the D notes).

Be careful of the rhythms here. Beat 1 is the shuffle rhythm, but beats 2–4 contain 16th-note hammer-ons. If you're having a hard time with the groove, remove the hammer-ons. Start by playing the shuffle rhythm on beat 1, followed by the three open E notes on beats 2–4. Once you're comfortable, add the hammer-on to beat 2, followed by two open E notes on beats 3–4. Progressively add the hammer-ons to beats 3 and 4 to complete the groove.

TRACK 131

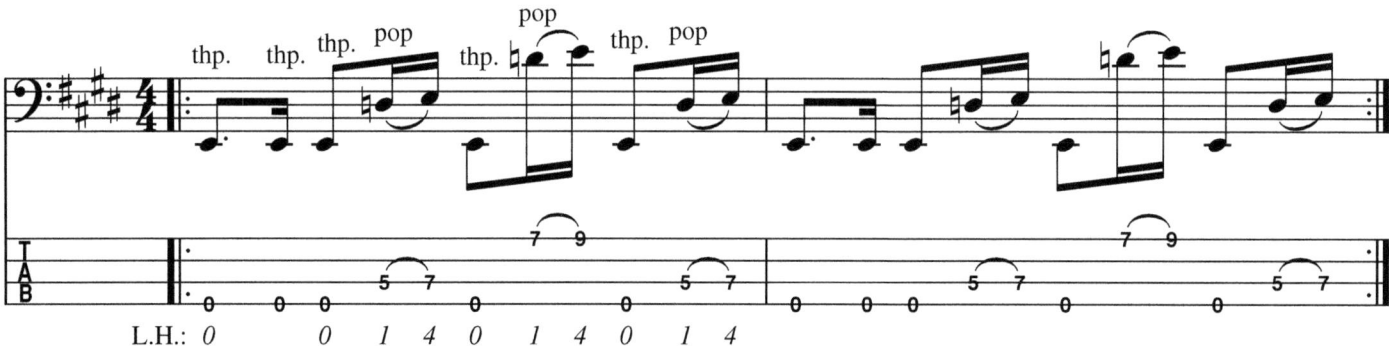

Slides

Sliding along the neck can be one of the most expressive tools for a bassist. The key to mastering a great slide is to *look at your target.* Let's play the open E string and slide up to the 12th fret on the same string. Keep your eye on the 12th fret while sliding up the neck—your hand will confidently stop right where you are looking! If you follow your hand as it slides up the neck, you'll miss the target. While sliding up the string, apply gentle pressure to create a smooth slide until you reach your target with full pressure.

In the following example, all of the slides are played with your 1st finger. Remember to look at the target fret. In measures 5, 6, and 8, there is a vibrato symbol (〜). Play the vibrato by rapidly bending and releasing the note. Bending the string a little gives a light vibrato; conversely, bending the sting excessively creates a wide and wild vibrato.

TRACK 132

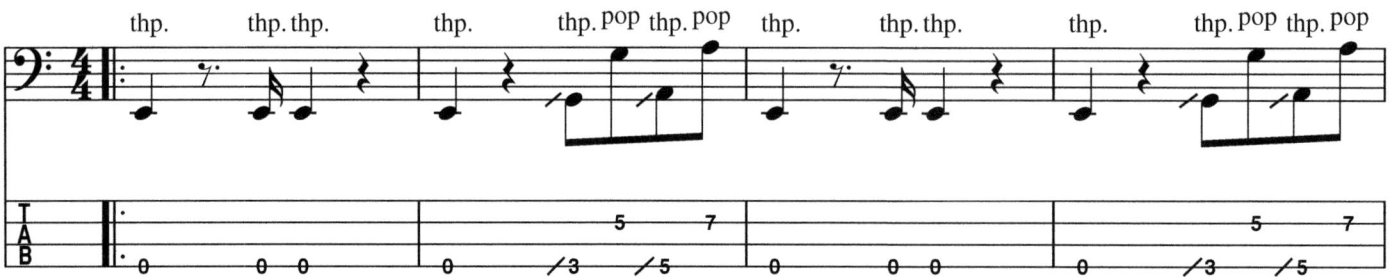

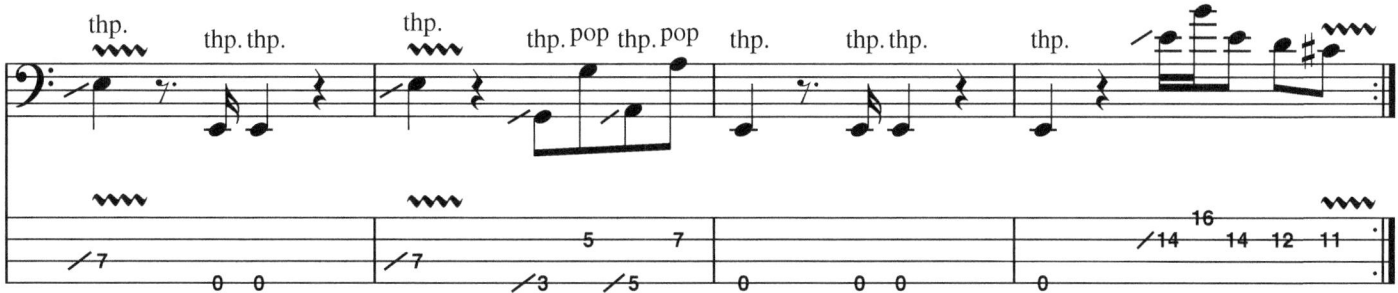

Using a slide can be a great way to move up or down the neck to play a fill. In the following example, quickly slide up the neck just after beat 2 in measures 2 and 4. Play the slides short, starting from about five frets below your target.

Start measure 2 with your 1st finger at the 1st fret and use it to slide up to the 13th fret. In measure 3, quickly return your 3rd finger to the 3rd fret. *Be careful not to slide back down the string to the 3rd fret.* Start measures 3–4 with your 3rd finger and use it to slide up to the 15th fret. Accent the last C with a short slide to restart the groove.

TRACK 133

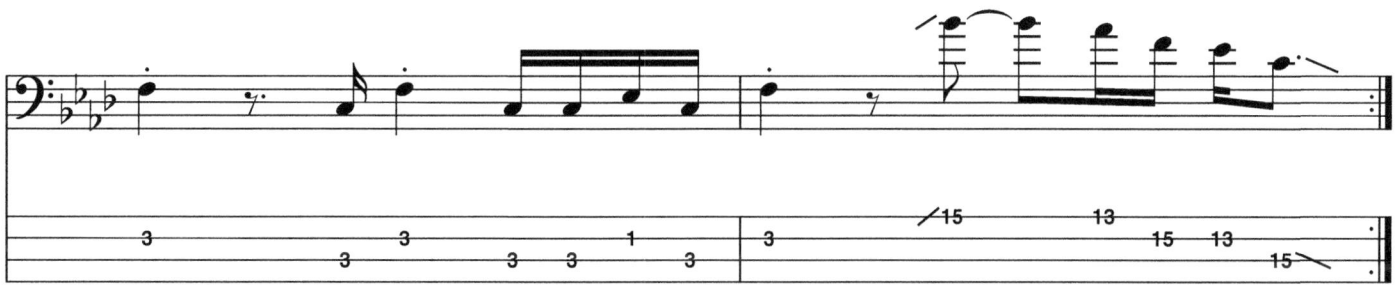

A Look at Minor Scales

Minor scales are different from major scales due to their order of half steps and whole steps. While major scales begin on "do," minor scales begin on "la." While there are several kinds of minor scales, the *natural minor scale* is one of the most common and is the one discussed here.

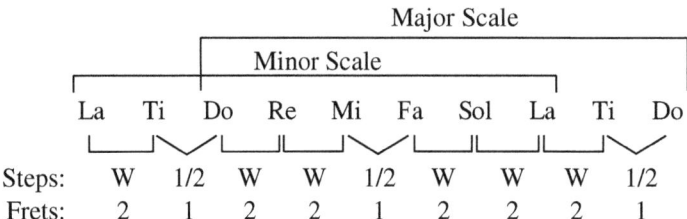

When a minor scale has the same number of sharps or flats as a major scale, the minor scale is said to be the "relative minor" of that major scale. The *key-note* (tonic) of a relative minor is found three half steps below that of the relative major. Another method of finding the relative minor is to count up the major scale six places (**C**–D–E–F–G–**A**–B–C). The relative minor of C major is A minor; the relative minor of G major is E minor; the relative minor of F major is D minor; etc. (Minor is usually abbreviated "min" or "m." Thus, A minor is often written as "Amin" or "Am," especially when referencing chord names.)

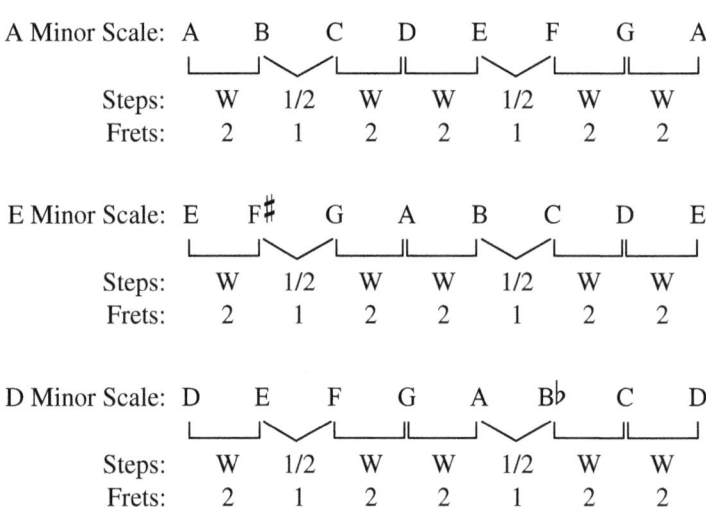

Relative-Minor Key Signatures

The key signatures for minor keys should be as familiar as those for the major keys. Here is a table to assist you in memorizing them.

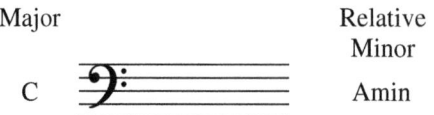

Relative-Minor Scales

The following are some of the relative-minor scales to practice. There are a few different fingerings, but they can be broken down into two categories. Just like the major scale, the minor scales can be played with open strings or with a movable pattern.

Open-String Fingerings

A minor contains no sharps or flats (the relative key of C major). Using the open strings, play through the scale. This is the familiar C major fret position from the beginning of the book. This pattern also can be moved to the E string to play an E minor scale.

TRACK 134

Movin' On Up: Movable Fingerings

If you move the A minor pattern up a half step, it creates the movable minor scale pattern. As with the major scale, it can be played on both the E and A strings. You should memorize this pattern. At the 1st fret, it is the B♭ minor and F minor scales.

TRACK 135   *B♭ Minor Scale*

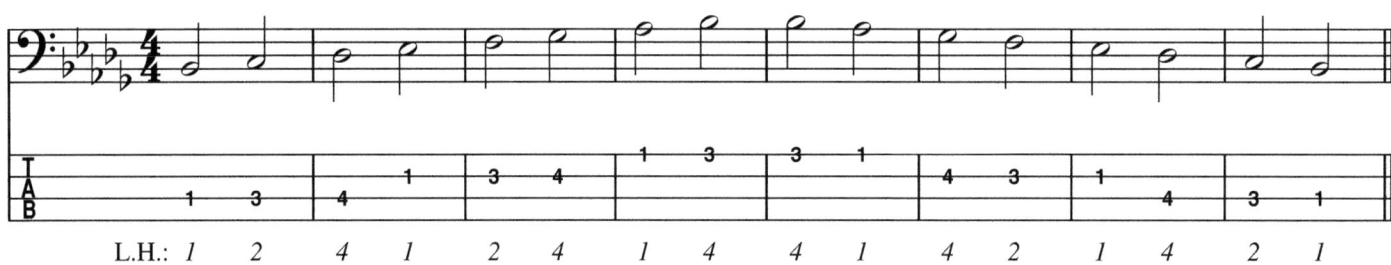

The following bass groove is based on the A minor and B♭ minor scales (note key change at end of second line). We'll use the same slide technique discussed earlier. On beat 4 of measure 7, quickly slide up to the 14th fret with your 2nd finger; this will allow you to play the high A on the G string with your 3rd finger. In measure 15, play the slide the same way—with your 2nd finger. Check out Earth, Wind, and Fire's "Kalimba Story."

TRACK 136

TRACK 137

F Minor Scale

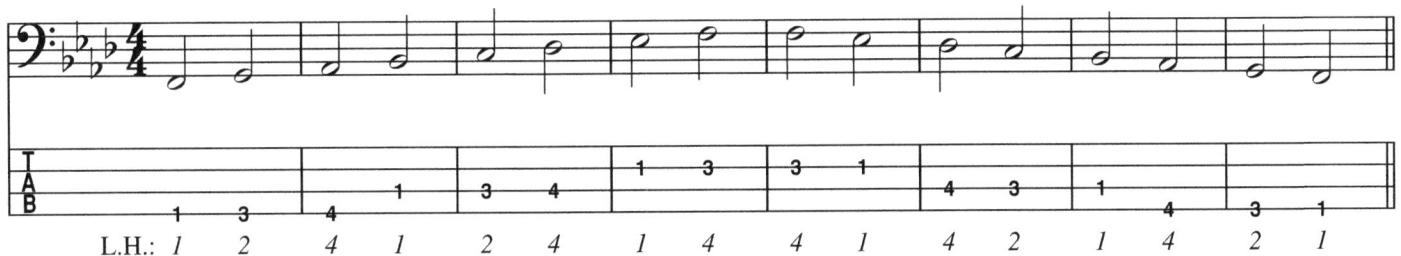

You can continue up each fret of the neck with the movable fingering to create all of the minor keys.

Using the Open Strings

At the 2nd fret, the B minor and F♯ minor scales also can be played with open strings.

TRACK 138 & 139

B Minor Scale

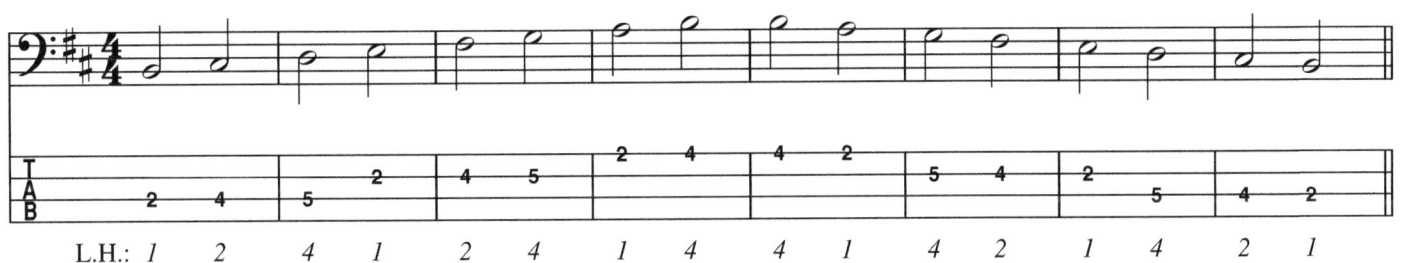

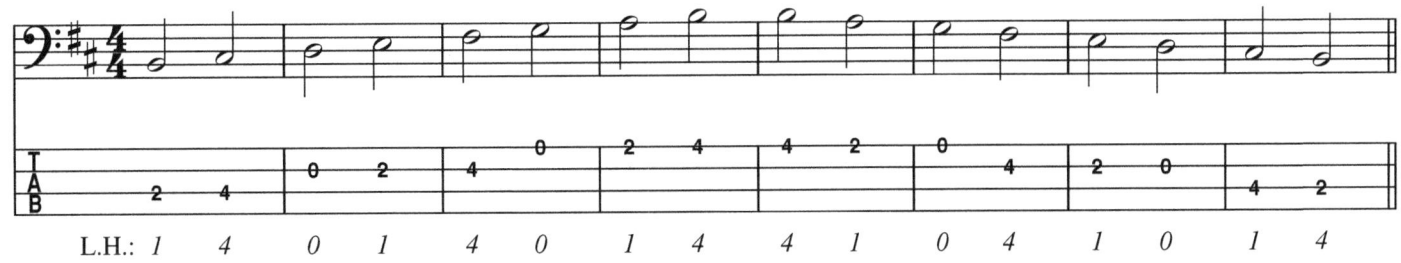

TRACK 140 & 141

F# Minor Scale

At the 3nd fret, the C minor and G minor scales also can be played with open strings.

TRACK 142 & 143

C Minor Scale

TRACK 144 & 145

G Minor Scale

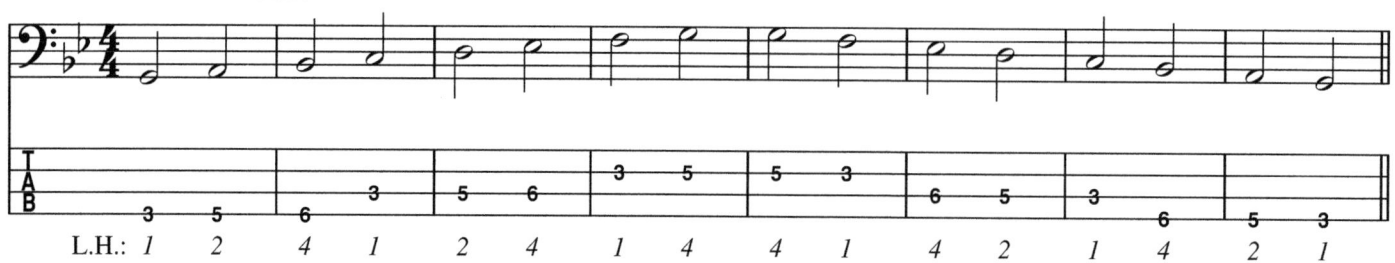

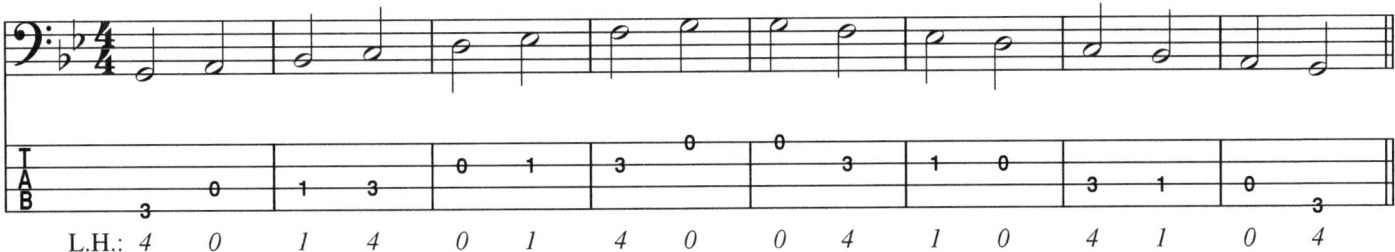

Movable Fingerings with a Shift

The A minor scale pattern also can be moved to the D string, but a shift will be necessary to play the scale. Shift up to the C on the G string with your 1st finger to complete the D minor scale. This fingering also can be moved down to the open A and E strings for an alternate A minor and E minor scale fingering.

TRACK 146

D Minor Scale

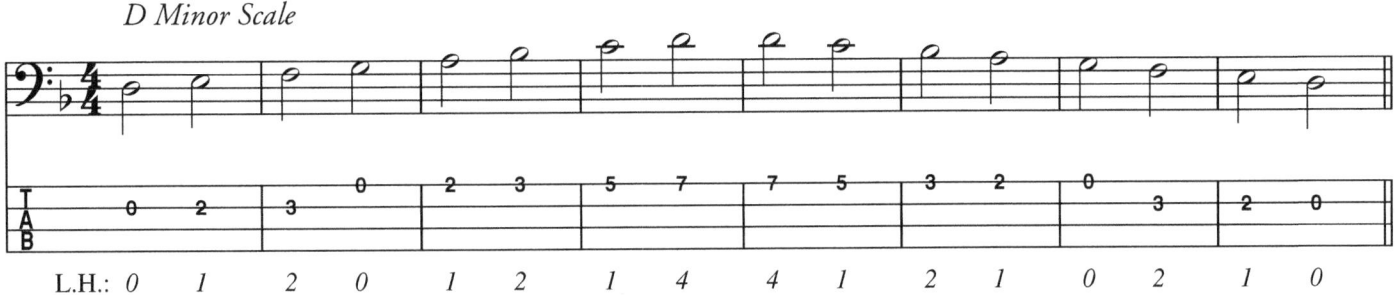

The two-octave E minor scale will shift up the A string to the second octave at the 7th fret.

TRACK 147

E Minor Scale

127

Strengthening the Fingers

The following arpeggio exercises will build your hand strength and give you confidence while moving across the neck. Play them slowly at first and focus on keeping your fingers close to the fretboard. If you're looking for a magic bullet to playing fast, this is the best place to start!

Major and Minor Arpeggio Exercises

This exercise is based on alternating ascending and descending major *arpeggios*—the notes of a chord played one after another instead of all at once. These major arpeggios are built on the first, third, fifth, and octave notes of a scale. The first arpeggio is an F major triad (F–A–C–F); the second is an F♯ (F♯–A♯–C♯–F♯); the third is G (G–B–D–G); etc.

The first arpeggio will use the open A string. On beat 3, use your 4th finger to shift from F to F♯. Play down the next arpeggio (F♯–C♯–A♯–F♯), and on the bottom F♯, use your 2nd finger to shift from F♯ to G. The fingerings and shifts will follow the same pattern for each new arpeggio. Remember to hold your 3rd and 4th fingers together while shifting to gain speed and accuracy.

TRACK 148

128

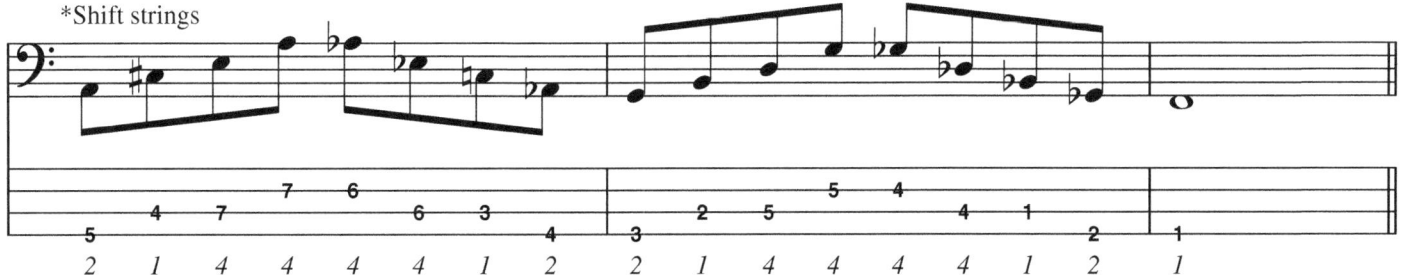

This exercise is the minor version of the previous exercise. It alternates ascending and descending minor triads. The first arpeggio is F minor—the third is now flat (F–**A♭**–C–F).

Start the F minor arpeggio (F–A♭–C–F) with your 1st finger, shifting up a half step with your 4th finger to the A♭ on the same string. The next two notes (C and F) will be right under your 2nd finger on the next two strings. Use your 2nd finger to shift up to the next arpeggio and reverse for the descending arpeggio. The fingering and shifts will remain the same as you move up the neck.

Make sure to *roll* your 2nd finger across the two notes on the same fret. A roll is performed by flattening out your finger to play notes on adjacent strings at the same fret.

TRACK 149

Verdine's Grooves

Verdine has personally recorded a couple of new grooves exclusively for the revised edition of this book! These grooves illustrate many of the elements discussed in this book, including syncopation, octaves, and playing across the neck.

This groove is based on a repeated one-bar phrase that's made up of open E's in beats 1 and 2, followed by a responding fretted fill in beats 3 and 4. Locking in to a repeated phrase on beat 1 is an essential part of creating good grooves of your own.

The groove begins with its fretted notes in 5th position. At the end of measure 4, make a quick shift to 7th position. In measure 11, shift up to 9th position for the high fill. Don't worry about getting back to the 5th fret; you'll have plenty of time to shift while playing the open E's before each fill.

There is some syncopation in this groove, so make sure you recognize the upbeats and downbeats in each measure. The groove gets real funky in measures 14–16, where Verdine leaves out the downbeat of beat 1! That's a great way to surprise the listener, but don't go dropping out beats randomly left and right. It only works if you first set the listener up to expect the beat.

In measures 7 and 23 there is a shake on the last B. A shake is like a vibrato, but instead of rapidly bending and releasing the note, you rapidly slide between two notes on the same string. If you listen closely, you can hear Verdine rapidly slide between B and C twice, returning to the B before the end of beat 4. Finally, remember to observe the staccato markings in each measure; they help keep the low notes from getting too muddy.

татк 150

Groove 1

Moderate Funk ♩ = 88

Like Groove 1, Groove 2 is built off a repeated rhythm in beats 1 and 2 of each measure. But now the groove is a two-bar phrase—so the fill is at the end of each second measure. From measure 5 on, the odd measures (5, 7, 9…) simply have quarter notes on beats 3 and 4, followed by busier fills on beats 3 and 4 of the even measures (6, 8, 10…). When creating your own grooves, use this alternation technique to add variety to your bass lines.

Start Groove 2 at the 14th fret with your 4th finger. Play the opening pickup notes just after beat 3 (on the second 16th note), and don't forget to play beat 4 short—as it is an eighth note. Most of the syncopation in the rest of this groove occurs in beats 1 and 2 on the open A string. If you're having trouble with the feel, listen to the accented bell sound in the percussion to help you lock in on the groove. After the opening pickup notes, shift to 5th position for the rest of the groove. Don't forget to observe the staccato markings; they add a punchy feel to the groove!

TRACK 151

Groove 2

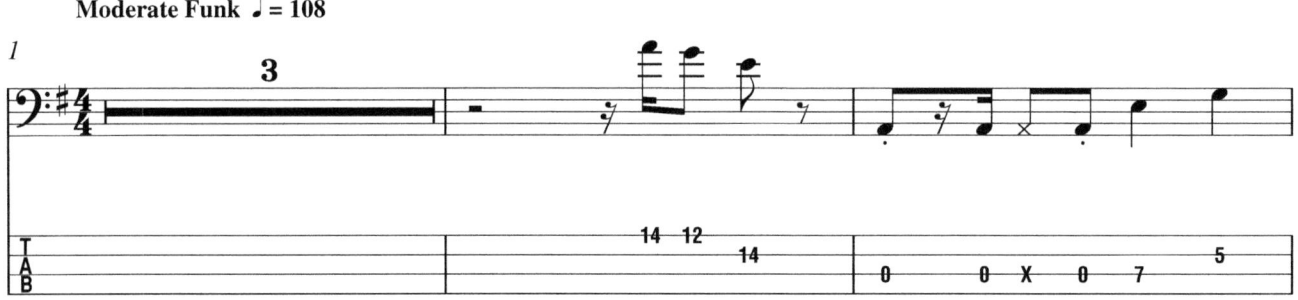

133

BUILD UP YOUR BASS CHOPS

100 FUNK/R&B LESSONS
Expand your bass knowledge with the Bass Lesson Goldmine series! Featuring 100 individual modules covering a giant array of topics, each lesson in this Funk/R&B volume includes detailed instruction with playing examples presented in standard notation and tablature. You'll also get extremely useful tips, scale diagrams, chord grids, photos, and more to reinforce your learning experience plus audio tracks featuring performance demos of all the examples in the book!
00131463 Book/Online Audio

BASS AEROBICS
by Jon Liebman
A 52-week, one-exercise-per-week workout program for developing, improving, and maintaining bass guitar technique. This book/audio combo will benefit all levels of players, from beginners to advanced, in all musical styles. The online audio includes demos as well as play-along grooves. By using this program you'll increase your speed, improve your dexterity and accuracy, heighten your coordination, and increase your groove vocabulary!
00696437 Book/Online Audio

BASS FRETBOARD ATLAS
by Joe Charupakorn
Mastering the bass neck has always been a challenge, even for very experienced players. The diagrams in *Bass Fretboard Atlas* will help you quickly memorize scales and arpeggios that may have previously seemed impossible to grasp. You'll be able to easily see and understand how scale and arpeggio shapes are laid out and how they connect and overlap across the neck.
00201827

BASSIST'S GUIDE TO SCALES OVER CHORDS
by Chad Johnson
With *Bassist's Guide to Scales Over Chords*, you'll learn how these two topics are intertwined in a logical and fundamental manner. This key concept is paramount in learning how to create and improvise functional and memorable bass lines or solos reliably time and again. This book includes 136 audio tracks and 17 extended backing tracks for download or streaming online.
00151930 Book/Online Audio

FRETBOARD ROADMAPS – BASS
by Fred Sokolow & Tim Emmons
This book/audio pack will get you playing bass lines anywhere on the fretboard, in any key. You'll learn to build bass lines under chord progressions; major, minor, and pentatonic scale patterns; and much more through easy-to-follow diagrams and instructions for beginning, intermediate, and advanced players. The online audio includes 64 demonstration and play-along tracks.
00695840 Book/Online Audio

LOUIS JOHNSON – BASS MASTER CLASS
For the first time, the legendary Louis Johnson "Star Licks" bass instruction videos are being made available in book format with online access to all the classic video footage. This package compiles Volumes I and II of the original Star Licks Master Classes into one bundle, giving you over an hour and a half of instruction, while the book contains transcriptions of every example played! All music is written in both standard notation and tab.
00156138 Book with Online Video

MUSIC THEORY FOR BASS PLAYERS
by Steve Gorenberg
With this comprehensive workbook, you'll expand your fretboard knowledge and gain the freedom and confidence needed to tackle any musical challenge. Features hundreds of examples to study and practice, including loads of "real world" bass lines and play-along audio tracks to jam to! Includes over 200 demonstration and play-along audio tracks and three bass fretboard theory video lessons online for download or streaming.
00197904 Book/Online Media

JACO PASTORIUS – BASS SIGNATURE LICKS
by Dan Towey
Learn the trademark grooves and solos of the man who revolutionized bass guitar. This book/online audio pack will help you take a closer look at Jaco's rich body of work through the structural, theoretical, and harmonic analysis of these classic recordings: Birdland • Come On, Come Over • Continuum • Liberty City • Night Passage • Palladium • and more!
00695544 Book/Online Audio

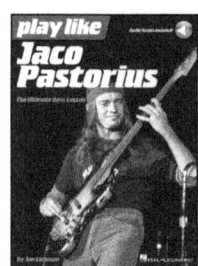

PLAY LIKE JACO PASTORIUS
THE ULTIMATE BASS LESSON
by Jon Liebman
Study the trademark songs, licks, tones and techniques of the world's greatest jazz fusion bassist, Jaco Pastorius.
This comprehensive book/audio teaching method provides detailed analysis of Pastoruis' gear, techniques, styles, songs, riffs and more. Each book comes with a unique code that will give you access to audio files of all the music in the book online. This pack looks at 15 of Jaco's most influential songs.
00128409 Book/Online Audio

STUFF! GOOD BASS PLAYERS SHOULD KNOW
by Glenn Letsch
Provides valuable tips on performing, recording, the music business, instruments and equipment (including electronics), grooves, fills, soloing techniques, care & maintenance, and more. Covers rock, jazz, blues, R&B and funk through demos of authentic grooves. The accompanying recordings include many of the examples in the book performed both in solo bass format and in a full-band setting so you can hear how important concepts fit in with other instruments and ensembles.
00696014 Book/Online Audio

WARM-UP EXERCISES FOR BASS GUITAR
by Steve Gorenberg
Bass players: customize your warm-up routine with this fantastic collection of stretches, coordination exercises, pentatonic scales, major and minor scales, and arpeggios sure to limber up your fingers and hands and get you ready to play in top form!
00148760

HAL•LEONARD®
www.halleonard.com

View our website for hundreds more bass books!

Prices, contents, and availability subject to change without notice.

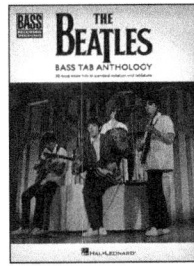

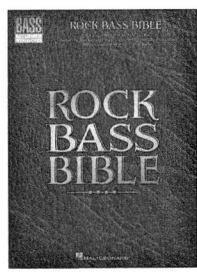
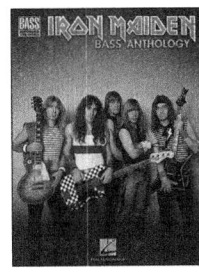

BASS RECORDED VERSIONS

Bass Recorded Versions feature authentic transcriptions written in standard notation and tablature for bass guitar.

25 Essential Rock Bass Classics
00690210

Avenged Sevenfold – Nightmare
00691054

The Beatles – Abbey Road
00128336

The Beatles – Bass Tab Anthology
01163910

The Beatles – 1962-1966
00690556

The Beatles – 1967-1970
00690557

Best of Bass Tab
00141806

The Best of Blink 182
00690549

Blues Bass Classics
00690291

Boston – Bass Collection
00690935

Stanley Clarke – Collection
00672307

Foo Fighters – Bass Tab Collection
00368888

Funk Bass Bible
00690744

Hard Rock Bass Bible
00690746

Jimi Hendrix – Are You Experienced?
00690371

Jimi Hendrix – Bass Tab Collection
00160505

Iron Maiden – Bass Anthology
00690867

Jazz Bass Classics
00102070

The Best of Kiss
00690080

Lynyrd Skynyrd – All-Time Greatest Hits
00690956

Bob Marley – Bass Collection
00690568

Mastodon – Crack the Skye
00691007

Megadeth – Bass Anthology
00691191

Metal Bass Tabs
00103358

Best of Marcus Miller
00690811

Motown Bass Classics
00690253

Muse – Bass Tab Collection
00123275

Nirvana – Bass Collection
00690066

Nothing More – Guitar & Bass Collection
00265439

The Essential Jaco Pastorius
00690420

Pearl Jam – Ten
00694882

Pink Floyd – Dark Side of the Moon
00660172

The Best of Police
00660207

Pop/Rock Bass Bible
00690747

Queen – The Bass Collection
00690065

R&B Bass Bible
00690745

Rage Against the Machine
00690248

Red Hot Chili Peppers – BloodSugarSexMagik
00690064

Red Hot Chili Peppers – By the Way
00690585

Red Hot Chili Peppers – Californication
00690390

Red Hot Chili Peppers – Greatest Hits
00690675

Red Hot Chili Peppers – I'm with You
00691167

Red Hot Chili Peppers – One Hot Minute
00690091

Red Hot Chili Peppers – Stadium Arcadium
00690853

Red Hot Chili Peppers – Unlimited Love
00905928

Rock Bass Bible
00690446

Royal Blood
00151826

Rush – The Spirit of Radio: Greatest Hits 1974-1987
00323856

Best of Billy Sheehan
00173972

Slap Bass Bible
00159716

Sly & The Family Stone for Bass
00109733

Sublime for Bass
00159716

Best of Yes
00103044

Best of ZZ Top for Bass
00691069

www.halleonard.com

Prices, contents & availability subject to change without notice. Some products may not be available outside the U.S.A.